Clicks well with others

$39⁹⁹

AirClick
Remote Control for iPod

- Control your iPod, iPod mini, or computer from up to 60 feet away
- Uses RF signals that travel through walls for remote control use anywhere in the house
- Tiny remote attaches to backpack, bike, steering wheel - anywhere for on-the-go control

$39⁹⁹

iTalk
iPod Voice Recorder

- Internal microphone and laptop quality speaker
- Connect external microphone or headphones
- Passthrough jack for headphones or additional speaker
- Automatic level control for perfect recordings

$14⁹⁹

LapelMic
Multi-use Stereo Microphone

- Self-powered microphone with stereo-quality sound
- Swivel clip for easy attachment
- Connects directly to iTalk, iMic, or PowerWave

$35

iTrip
FM Transmitter for iPod

- The only FM Transmitter designed exclusively for the iPod & iPod mini
- Powered from the iPod - no batteries necessary
- Choose any empty station from 87.7 to 107.9, and change your iTrip stations directly from the iPod

$19⁹⁹

TuneJuice
Battery Backup for iPod and iPod mini

- Provides up to 8 hours of additional power to iPod
- Uses any disposable or rechargeable 9-volt battery
- Carry emergency iPod power wherever you go
- Works with any dockable iPod or iPod mini

Made for iPod

- Made for iPod mini
- Made for iPod Photo
- Made for 4th Generation iPod with Click Wheel
- Made for 3rd Generation iPod with touch wheel and buttons

Buy now at **www.GRIFFINtechnology.com**

Another great idea from **GRIFFIN**

Make:
technology on your time™

Volume 02

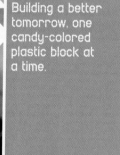

Building a better tomorrow, one candy-colored plastic block at a time.

Puppy love: Transforming abandoned toys into environmental avengers.

ON THE COVER
Photographer Dan Goldberg enjoyed the "amazing work" of these extreme Star Wars cloners. Read all about these diehard fans and their creations on page 160.
(Tom Jozwiak and his creation, at right)

Increase Your
Security Muscle

Strengthen your defenses. Train your mind. Learn the threats of tomorrow, today.
Be challenged by the experts who are doing innovative work. Meet and network with
thousands of your peers from all corners of the world at the Black Hat Briefings USA 2005–
the only technical security event to offer you the best of all worlds.

Black Hat®
Briefings & Training USA 2005
July 23-28, 2005 • Caesars Palace Las Vegas
Training: 4 days, 25 topics • Briefings: 2 days, 10 tracks, 60 speakers

www.blackhat.com
for updates and to register.

Make: Projects

Atari 2600PC
Mod the classic game console to play hundreds of retro-game titles and DVDs. By Joe Grand

Podcasting 101
Record and distribute your audio over the internet. By Phillip Torrone

Mousey the Junkbot
With a few spare parts, you can turn an old computer mouse into an amusing little robot.
By Gareth Branwyn

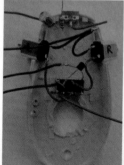

This Old Amp
Restore an old guitar amplifier and make it sound as good or better than the day it was made.
By Tom and Wendell Anderson

Volume 02

Learning a watchmaker's skills will give you hours of fun.

DIY

Peeping zoom: Turn your webcam into a daytime telescope.

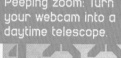

Mark Frauenfelder

WHEN USERS MAKE

I'VE BEEN READING TWO BOOKS THAT SEEM, at least on the surface, to be unrelated. One is called *Thoughtless Acts* (Chronicle Books, 2005), written by Jane Fulton Suri, who runs the human factors R&D department at the design consultancy IDEO. (The book also happens to have been handsomely designed by MAKE's own creative director, David Alberston.) It's collection of 160 candid street photographs taken of people adapting to, reacting to, and making use of things in the natural and designed world. The book's title describes the way people come up with clever solutions to everyday problems without really thinking about them. Examples include winding a tea bag string through a cup handle to keep the tag from falling in the cup, sticking a pencil in your hair for easy access, and covering a broken parking meter with a paper bag.

The other book is called *Democratizing Innovation* (MIT Press, 2005) by Eric von Hippel, a professor and head of the Innovation and Entrepreneurship Group at the MIT Sloan School of Management. Von Hippel argues that individuals have stopped becoming mere consumers of mass-produced products and are now contributing to the development of new products. We've seen this happen with open source software; open source hardware is the next phase.

Extreme sports equipment is a good example of the democratizing of innovation. "Lead users" in windsurfing, mountain biking, and board sports lead the way in improving equipment, sometimes using the open source software model to develop and refine their innovations.

These two books are related because they represent opposite ends of the same spectrum. Both explore people's natural urge to make things, whether it's a doorstop from a wine bottle cork, or a special chemical etchant that a rock climber can use to cut a trapped rope.

Innovation isn't only about making your own products from scratch; it's also about customizing the technology you already own to suit your needs. The theme of this issue is "home entertainment," and if ever a category of technology were in need of customizing, this is it. Sadly, consumer electronics manufacturers have kowtowed to the overreaching demands of entertainment companies to lock up their products and prevent people from infringing on their copyrights. It's fine for a company to protect its intellectual property, but there are already plenty of laws to protect them and punish the guilty. In addition to the draconian penalties it's seduced Congress into legislating, Hollywood is also threatening hardware manufacturers into crippling the functionality of game, video, and music players. Why can't you back up a DVD to your hard drive or copy it to your handheld computer? It's because Hollywood won't allow it.

Yankee Ingenuity — that is, improvising with technology, taking ownership of it, and being self-reliant and creative with it — is a proud American tradition that has spread to every corner of the free world. Hollywood's efforts to impose Soviet-style centralized control on technology are a huge step backwards for innovation. As security consultant Bruce Schneier so aptly put it, the entertainment companies are "willing to destroy your privacy, have general-purpose computers declared illegal, and exercise special vigilante police powers that no one else has, just to make sure that no one watches *The Little Mermaid* without paying for it."

In this issue, we look at the restrictions the entertainment industry has imposed on equipment, and we show you some ways to uncripple your video recorder, your music player, and your game console.

It's not that we're in favor of breaking laws or stealing other people's property. We're not. But we are interested in finding ways to make the technology we own better. We suspect you are, too.

Mark Frauenfelder (markf@oreilly.com) is editor-in-chief of MAKE.

Make:
technology on your time™

EDITOR AND PUBLISHER
Dale Dougherty
dale@oreilly.com

EDITOR-IN-CHIEF
Mark Frauenfelder
markf@oreilly.com

CREATIVE DIRECTOR
David Albertson
david@albertsondesign.com

MANAGING EDITOR
Shawn Connally
shawn@oreilly.com

ART DIRECTOR
Kirk von Rohr

ASSOCIATE EDITOR
Phillip Torrone
pt@makezine.com

ASSOCIATE PUBLISHER, MARKETING
Dan Woods

PROJECTS EDITOR
Paul Spinrad
pspinrad@makezine.com

ADVERTISING DIRECTOR
Bill Takacs
707-827-7092, bill@oreilly.com

EDITORIAL ASSISTANT
Arwen O'Reilly

ADVERTISING COORDINATOR
Jessica Boyd

COPY CHIEF
Goli Mohammadi

PUBLISHER AT LARGE
John Battelle

COPY EDITORS/RESEARCH
Sarah Saulsbury
Michael Shapiro

PUBLISHED BY O'REILLY MEDIA, INC.
Tim O'Reilly, CEO
Laura Baldwin, COO

WEBMASTER
Terrie Miller

WEB DESIGN
Laura Schmier

Visit us online at:
makezine.com

MAKE TECHNICAL ADVISORY BOARD:
**Gareth Branwyn, Joe Grand,
Saul Griffith, Natalie Jeremijenko**

Contributors

Andrew Argyle (*Primer*) describes himself as "an intelligent biped" who enjoys taking things apart as much as putting them back together. He's working on making a USB-to-serial/parallel converter, a Geiger counter, and a bead loom for one of his sisters, as well as playing ball hockey, growing exotic cacti from seed, and playing acoustic blues guitar. He did support for the Unix and Linux versions of WordPerfect, was part of the development team for Corel Linux, and has worked for internet startups. He lives in deep suburbia with his wife and stepdaughter.

Gareth Branwyn (*Mousey*) is something of a reluctant geek ("I'm more of an arty-farty type and a journalist."). This doesn't stop him from being endlessly fascinated by all forms of technology, especially their application outside of any intended purpose. He is "Cyborg-in-Chief" of Streettech.com and recently co-wrote a book on TiVo hacking, *Leo Laporte's Guide to TiVo*. He lives in Arlington, Virg., with his 17-year-old son, and has been trying to make robots since he was 6 years old, when he told his cousin that he'd made a robot to do his chores.

Erica Sadun (*HDTV on Your Mac*) has written, co-written, and contributed to almost two dozen books about technology, particularly in the areas of Programming, Digital Video, and Digital Photography. An unrepentant geek, Sadun has never met a gadget she didn't need. Her checkered past includes run-ins with NeXT, Newton, and a vast myriad of successful and unsuccessful technologies. When not writing, she and her geek husband parent three adorable geeks-in-training, who regard their parents with restrained bemusement.

Tom and Wendell Anderson (*This Old Amp* and *irock Broadcast Boombox*) are descended from generations of engineers. Inspired by their dad, they each started engineering at 13, doing electronics piecework in their basement. In their spare time they snowboard, build stuff, play music, program, and design analog circuits. Despite the implication of this bio, they are not twins.

Dan Goldberg (*R2-DIY*) thoroughly enjoyed shooting the Star Wars story. A passionate photographer who has worked with MAKE designers on other stories for (gasp!) other magazines, he is also working on a personal project about WWII vets. "I am always photographing something different, which brings fresh new challenges and excitement," he says. He likes to fly-fish, hike, camp, and just generally enjoy the outdoors every chance he gets. He lives in Chicago with his wife, illustrator Casey Lukatz. He does not like the color purple.

"I still can't quite believe that I can actually be paid money to draw," says **Damien Scogin** (illustrator of MAKE's DIY section). With grandparents who taught him drawing techniques at age 5 and a photographer father, Damien has been living and breathing art for his entire life. His favorite fruit is the banana, and he is currently very smitten with dark brown and light green. He lives near beautiful Lake Merritt in Oakland with his girlfriend and spends his spare time dreaming about backpacking trips in California's High Sierra.

Contributing Writers:
Tim Anderson, Tom Anderson, Wendell Anderson, Andrew Argyle, Dennison Bertram, Adam Bernard, Gareth Branwyn, Mark R. Brown, Richard Butner, Simon Carless, Mike Chambers, John Clark, Cory Doctorow, Joshua Ellis, Craig Engler, Elliot C. Evans, Limor Fried, Joe Grand, Saul Griffith, Benjamin Heckendorn, John Irvine, Xeni Jardin, Stefan Jones, Adam W. Kempa, Jason Kottke, Brian Lawler, William Lidwell, Merlin Mann, Michael McDonald, Danny O'Brien, Aleks Oniszcsak, Tim O'Reilly, Tom Owad, Ross Orr, Bob Parks, Erica Sadun, Bob Scott, Bruce Sterling, Adam Thornton, Marc Weidenbaum, Howard Wen, Ben Wheeler, Zach Slootsky

Contributing Artists:
Nick Dragotta, Noelle Gaberman, Dan Goldberg, Sara Huston, Timmy Kucynda, Tim Lillis, Topher Lucas, Emily Nathan, Damien Scogin, Nik Schulz, Derrick Story

FOCUS

OR, WHY YOUR WEB BROWSER NEEDS A HYPOTHALAMUS

By Merlin Mann & Danny O'Brien

TIME

suggests that it's creative people like yourself who seem to have the worst time staying focused on their work.

Now, far be it from us to imply that MAKE has somehow contributed to your personal procrastination problem; you may, in fact, have a variety of work-related projects that will benefit from that new kitty-cat jetpack. But if your boss is tapping her foot and staring at her watch, you might consider a few tricks for getting back on track.

For most garden-variety procrastinators, just removing a few strategic distractions can reclaim focus. Chances are, you already know your distractions better than you'd like to admit. Maybe it's AIM, IRC, talk radio, or that scrumptious stream of KEXP. Start by dumping anything that proves to be an attractive nuisance for the part of your brain that needs to think just about the work at hand. You're the best judge of what you need to keep your project moving forward, but the easiest solution may be the most primitive: unplug the router.

If you need internet access for what you're doing but can't risk falling into a four-hour, unchaperoned surfin' safari, try some localized hacking. One popular trick around the lab is to set up a Perl-based web proxy that watches for 15 contiguous minutes of web browsing, then throws a gentle pop-up window to ask if you're still just looking for that one piece of information you claim to be searching for. (Watch 43folders.com for a link to download this proxy.)

If that devil, AIM, has to be on for your work, consider getting an account with IM Smarter (imsmarter.com). It's an AIM proxy that lets you build your own electronic scold. Once configured, you can, among other things, IM their smart little robot (AIM:imsmarter) with a request like "remind me in 15 minutes to quit reading Slashdot." It obliges by directing your attention back to work.

A favorite nag for all seasons is the humble, digital kitchen timer. You can pick one up for $5 at any drugstore. Try setting it for 5, 8, or 15 minutes — whatever you consider the maximum amount of squandered time you can afford to lose today — and when it starts beeping at you, get the hell back to work. This can also be useful for "sprints," where you make a deal with yourself to go heads-down for 15 or 30 minutes of dedicated work in return for the Skinnerian pellet of your choice.

If you prefer more cerebral approaches to your problem — and God knows, most procrastinators think they do — you can try some mental tricks that help alleviate the anxieties and mounting pressure that are making your delaying tactics kick in.

In his popular essay, "Structured Procrastination" (xrl.us/procrastination), John Perry posits that procrastination is caused by an inability to finish the most important items on your To-Do list. He suggests creating tasks that seem important and urgent (but really aren't) and then moving them to the top of your list. Since experienced procrastinators find self-deception second nature, they can usually psych themselves into getting something accomplished just by pretending it's not that important.

> "For most procrastinators, removing a few strategic distractions can allow you to reclaim focus."

We are partial, though, to the inverse model of procrastination espoused by Joshua Bryce Newman (xrl.us/kickstart), who suggests scheduling regular, short bursts of work surrounded by much larger blocks of deliberate non-work. Give yourself a five minute task starting at 9 a.m., then get right back to playing Galaga at 9:05. As Joshua notes, removing that pressure and guilt can sometimes lead to an impressive "productivity surge."

Speaking of "productivity," it's time we all admit that the biggest time burglar of them all is excessive meta-work like rearranging your Day Runner, moving your mail around in Outlook, or fiddling with the endless lists that are meant to help you with Getting Things Done.

Life Hacks Labs has learned that the cardinal rule of productivity cults can be rather painful in its Zen-slappingness: if you're spending more time thinking about your work than you are doing it, you're not being particularly productive.

Whenever you feel the bug to stop working and go play with your "system," fight it off or make it into a reward for reaching a milestone. But don't let it replace the real work you have in front of you.

Learn how to reel in your mind at Danny O'Brien's *lifehacks. com* and Merlin Mann's *43folders.com*.

Tim O'Reilly

NEWS FROM THE FUTURE

"The future is here. It's just not evenly distributed yet." — William Gibson

ONE OF THE BEST PIECES OF ADVICE I ever received when my kids were young was this: "Your job as a parent is to prepare your children for their future." For *their* future, not the one that you grew into — that's their past. So when my kids got old enough to be interested, I started News From the Future as a private mailing list for them and their friends, wanting to send them stories that I thought might help prepare them for what may come. But it's also great grist for a stream-of-consciousness news feed in the style of *Harper's Weekly*! In that spirit, here are some headlines from recent news stories....

Korean roboticist Kim Jong-Hwan has developed "artificial chromosomes" he says will allow robots to feel lusty, and could eventually lead them to reproduce. UK researchers have developed a computer that was able to learn "rock, paper, scissors" by watching humans play the game, and at the University of Bath, a tiny sensor drone powers itself by feeding on dead flies. A University of Minnesota team has constructed synthetic DNA that could be used to direct the assembly of computer circuits. Meanwhile, some Lexus cars may be vulnerable to infection by a virus transmitted via Bluetooth from mobile phones.

New Orleans is experimenting with IP-based surveillance cameras on a wireless mesh network in high-crime neighborhoods. A new service uses cellphone location to track how fast teens are driving, and sends alerts back to parents, while California is entertaining proposals to require GPS in all cars so that it can tax miles driven rather than gasoline used. China plans to launch 100 surveillance satellites by 2020. But the surveillance society won't be without its countermeasures, and its rats hiding in the walls. HP just received a patent on a system for broadcasting an "image inhibitor" signal that would fuzz facial images captured by a digital camera.

Never mind outsourcing — the spread of GPS navigation systems is leading to the closure of lighthouses along the German coast. Meanwhile, imaginary worlds are big business: traffic in LA was snarled as thousands tried to get to a new-release event with the creators of the World of Warcraft MMORPG. Maria Schneider won a Grammy for an album financed by her fans and distributed only on the web. A Seattle supermarket introduced a "pay by fingerprint" service, and Alaskan researchers created an artificial aurora they say might one day be useful for writing advertising messages on the night sky.

Scientists at the University of Manchester have developed an inkjet printer that can print human cells, and a Chicago chef prints out flavored-paper sushi. Ophthalmologists at Rush University Medical Center implanted artificial silicon retina microchips in the eyes of five patients, and in San Diego, researchers plan to hold an arm-wrestling match between a human being and an artificial arm made from electroactive polymers. A Utah State University professor plans RFID-equipped robots to guide blind people to products in the supermarket. And a company in Los Angeles is taking orders for genetically engineered hypo-allergenic cats. Freeman Dyson wonders if we're ending the "Darwinian interlude."

At MIT, a space elevator prototype successfully climbed a 260-foot building. A group of amateur astronomers processed the raw images of Titan from the Huygens probe faster than the official space agencies. A new solar-sail design could theoretically reach Mars in a month. NASA is looking at commercial alternatives for space-station resupply, and a private space-flight bill was signed into law.

Seen signs of a future not yet widely distributed? Report news from the future to nff@makezine.com. To sign up for the News From the Future mailing list, send email to join-nff@newsletter.oreilly.com. You can get URLs for the referenced stories at makezine.com/02/nff.

Tim O'Reilly (*tim.oreilly.com*) is the founder and CEO of O'Reilly Media, Inc.

Insect Inside

Garnet Hertz will never want or need to debug his mobile robot, because it's controlled by a live cockroach. Fastened into the three-wheeled vehicle via velcro cemented to its back, the bug drives by moving a ping-pong ball under its feet. The ball fits into the workings of a Kensington trackball, turned 45 degrees so that its two axes correspond to angled-left and angled-right, rather than horizontal and vertical. The movements are then decoded and amplified by transistors to drive left and right rear wheels, which turn in slightly to reflect the roach's steering direction.

Power comes from twin 24-volt DC motors and a 24-volt battery. Meanwhile, four infrared proximity sensors surround the front of the vehicle and switch on a row of LEDs that shine in the roach's eyes when the vehicle approaches an object. Because cockroaches avoid light, this is intended to discourage the robot from bumping into things. But if the

insect evaluates the distance it travels based on the length of its unenhanced stride, it's possible that when its steps are greatly amplified — as they are when it is placed in the robot — its ability to navigate will be impaired.

The bug buggy's CPU is a Giant Madagascan Hissing Cockroach (*Gromphadorhina portentosa*). Hertz has worked with the species before, and it's well suited to such applications. Their size and strength let them move relatively large objects, and their native forest-floor habitat makes them well suited to being literally pressed into service. Working with insects requires no animal ethics procedures or approvals, unlike with mammals, and anyway, if you mistreat *G. portentosa*, it will hiss loudly. Cockroaches in general, meanwhile, carry a pile of personal and cultural associations. Everyone has had their own vivid experiences with the Kafkaesque insects, and this just adds to the fun.

Photography by Garnet Hertz

Hertz is most interested in how the cockroach does *not* act like a computer chip, how its behavior defies easy logic. Watching the roachbot cruise along at slow walking speed, stumbling and bumping into things, it's impossible not to wonder about the underlying neural processes, which propagate through a distributed set of ganglia rather than a central brain. On another level, the robot system is meant to be funny, but some also see it as a dark reduction of human-machine interaction. Following this theme, Hertz's paper describing the project, "Control and Communication in the Animal and the Machine," takes its name from the subtitle of Norbert Wiener's seminal 1948 book, *Cybernetics*.

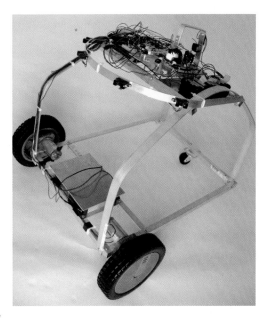

Hertz first demonstrated his roachmobile at last year's SIGGRAPH, where it milled around the audience during the conference's popular wearable-computing fashion show. At this year's SIGGRAPH, however, Hertz feels that his state-of-the-art roach couture may be ready for the runway.

—*Paul Spinrad*

≫ Control and Communication in the Animal and the
Machine: *conceptlab.com/control*

15-Mile-High Club

Forget billionaire Richard Branson's overpriced tourist spaceships. For a few thousand bucks, physics student **Art Vanden Berg** put his computer-controlled model glider 79,000 feet into the stratosphere. This summer, he plans to launch a second prototype even higher.

The ill-fated test craft had a wingspan of about four feet, weighed about six pounds, and achieved its high altitudes when carried by helium-filled weather balloons. A glider is much more versatile than other payloads, which often depend on parachutes to fall to Earth. Vanden Berg's craft remained aloft for up to four hours, snapping beautiful, low-res color pics the whole time. "Above 60,000 feet the Earth has a definite curvature; the temperature's around -50 degrees Celsius [-58° F], and the sky is black because you're above most of the atmosphere," notes the native of Victoria, Canada. And most of the time, the plane flew right back to the launch site.

For a pilotless craft, the fiberglass and spruce shell hid a lot of smarts. A fist-size 25-MHz PC in the fuselage ran DOS and over 13,000 lines of code that Vanden Berg lovingly programmed himself in C. The operator could provide manual control via the radio link, but the glider usually flew autonomously using a large set of software decision trees. Position and flight data streamed into the system from a Garmin GPS sensor and sensors for temperature, direction, G-load, and airspeed. The glider sent real-time photos and atmospheric readings to the ground using a packet-radio with a 120-mile range.

On its fifth and last journey, the glider couldn't quite clear a snowy mountain peak nearly 60 miles from the launch site. "It was actually good luck because now I can build a really *skookum* glider," says Vanden Berg, employing local slang for "cool." He now has a new airframe at almost half the weight and a good chance at pulling images from 89,000 feet above the surface of the Earth.

—*Bob Parks*

≫ **High Altitude Glider:** *members.shaw.ca/sonde/*

Photograph by Simon Brink

Smashing Success

With big, expensive equipment and closely controlled experiment schedules, particle physics has never been a field for the do-it-yourselfer. But that didn't stop **Tim Koeth** from building two operational cyclotrons on his own time and dime. Koeth began the project as an undergrad physics major at Rutgers University, soon after learning how the machines worked, at least in theory. Koeth and his friend Stuart Hanebuth worked on the atom-smashers for several years and saw their first proton beam in 1999; now the devices are permanent fixtures in the physics department and part of Rutgers' standard senior lab curriculum.

The cyclotrons are named for the pole diameters of their water-cooled electromagnets: there's the 9-inch and the 12-inch. Most of the parts for both were scrounged, bought used for cheap, or custom-fabricated at the university machine shop. The 12-inch cyclotron uses a 2.5-ton magnet that came from Argonne National Laboratory, where it had been the steering magnet for a decommissioned accelerator. The vacuum chambers and the cylindrical vessel

positioned between the poles where all the action takes place were fabbed out of stainless steel, with Viton synthetic rubber O-ring seals and an off-the-shelf diffusion pump.

When the 12-inch cyclotron runs, hydrogen from an outside tank slowly leaks through a pipe into a small ceramic cup in the center of the chamber. Inside the cup, a glowing electric filament splits the hydrogen ions, a.k.a. protons, away from their electrons. (Don't try this at home, unless your home has no oxygen.) Meantime, square-wave AC runs through the electromagnet, producing a shifting field that's precisely timed using grad-school equations to accelerate the ions in an ever-faster spiral outward. The much lighter electrons are immediately swept far off in the opposite direction and absorbed by the apparatus, which is grounded. In other experiments deuterium replaces hydrogen, and the magnetic field is timed to accelerate a proton-neutron pair rather than a single proton.

At the end of its acceleration, the beam is interrupted and detected by instruments inside the vacuum chamber. Getting the beam to exit would require an electrostatic projector to peel particles away from their orbits, and a thin Kevlar seal over the port to maintain the vacuum while letting high-energy particles pass through.

Koeth's success demonstrates that no physics project, no matter how advanced, is beyond the capability of creative and determined college students. Let that be an inspiration, and a warning.

—Paul Spinrad

≫ **Rutgers University Cyclotron:**
www.physics.rutgers.edu/cyclotron

SunVee

With the peak oil crisis looming, the Vee 9 solar vehicle has been getting a lot of press recently. And for good reason — it promises the same guilt-free commute experience as trendier rides like the Toyota Prius and Ford Escape — but for nearly $20,000 less.

However, DIY does mean you have to build it yourself. And don't expect to see Cameron Diaz tooling around Hollywood in one any time soon: the boxy bio-auto bears large panels for collecting ambient light, and resembles a "what-if-they-mated" mash up between a Coney Island go-kart and a Burning Man art car.

Funny appearance aside, the Vee 9 is the product of serious engineering smarts. Canadian developers **Jeff Dekzty** and **Will Scully** designed the two-seater to be built easily from a list of parts totaling a mere $1,600. Required components include about 200 cellphone batteries, commercially available solar panels, and a 500-watt magnetic hub.

With a maximum load of 300 pounds and a clearance range of 7 feet, the vehicle carries 2 people, or 1 person and an ample load of groceries. It can reach speeds of up to 21 miles per hour.

But in true, open source tradition, the vehicle's co-creators welcome design improvements or variations from other tinkerers. What they ask in return is simple: just let them know what you learned.

The duo claims to have driven the Vee 9 for trips of up to 170 miles. Each of those trips required an hour-long recharge stop. Among the words of wisdom you'll find on their solarvehicles.org site is a hilarious FAQ with answers to questions like, "How far can you go before needing to recharge the batteries?" Their response: "This is not [a question] for Light-Driven Vehicles ... which are plugged into the sun."

—*Xeni Jardin*

≫ **Plans and part lists are available online at** *solarvehicles. org/pages/3/*, **and there's a group for likeminded builders at** *groups.msn.com/BioMod/*.

Photograph by Jeff Dekzty

Batching It

Like many of us, **Matthias Wandel** spent a lot of time robotically swapping disks in and out of his CD burner, ripping music, and doing backups. Then he thought he could rig up something to perform the tasks for him. He was right. By pulling together some electronics design, mechanics, coding, and woodworking, Wandel built a Linux PC-controlled contraption that rips through stacks of CDs.

A hinged wooden finger opens and closes via solenoid, conveying the CDs by grabbing and releasing them by their centerholes. Motorized pulleys move the grabber. This CD transport mechanism is run by an external controller board full of solid-state relays, retired lab equipment that Wandel bought at a University of Waterloo surplus sale. The relays act as a bridge between the Linux machine and the mechanicals, translating digital commands from the computer's printer port into motor-capable voltages.

CD burner functions are done with the standard Linux utility cdrecord. By making calls to cdrecord and his own C routines, Wandel can load, rip, and stack CDs from the command line and run batch jobs by calling a simple shell script. In other words, the whole thing works. But now, after having proven the concept, he's partially dismantled the contraption. He wants to use those solid-state relays for some other projects he's been thinking about.

—*Paul Spinrad*

≫ **Matthias Wandel:** *sentex.net/~mwandel*

AlternaJets

Talk about cheap transportation — how about a jet engine made from a couple of commuter coffee mugs and a sink strainer? Amateur designer **Larry Cottrill** welded the parts together after realizing that the cups' graceful lines form the perfect shape for what's known as a "ramjet," a jet engine that uses moving air to compress volatile gases.

This Starbucks-inspired idea could be space-aged or simply spaced-out, but Cottrill plans to test his creation this summer. Meanwhile, the Iowa-based inventor has earned serious cred for his designs on an online forum for exotic engines, pulse-jets.com. It's a site populated by hobbyists looking for alternatives to expensive turbine engines currently available for model airplanes.

A prolific designer of mongrel flyers, Cottrill recently wowed the online forums with a blueprint for a "focused-wave valveless pulsejet." The basic design has been around since World War II. Cottrill's setup makes strides in the affordability of materials, simplicity of design, and the thrust of the engine. It was successfully constructed in 2004 by hobbyists in Connecticut and Pennsylvania, and by Cottrill himself, who says the sound was so loud he needed a set of plastic ear muffs over his foam ear plugs. "There's really nothing like a pulsejet. It roars much louder than a diesel train whistle; it's unbelievable."

—*Bob Parks*

≫ **Coffee Mug Ramjet:**
cottrillcyclodyne.com/Maggie_Muggs/Maggie.html

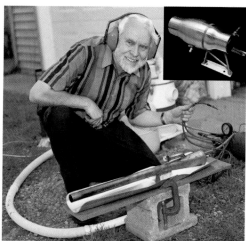

Lego Type

In the days before digital type, fonts were often distributed on two-inch film reels for use with photo-typesetting machines like the VGC Photo-Typositor. Mark Simonson, a Twin Cities-based type designer, is working to convert some of the film fonts done by prolific type designer Phil Martin to digital formats.

A flatbed scanner and standard filmstrip holder were employed in the digitizing process, but Simonson needed a spooling mechanism to keep the film from flopping about and getting scratched. To solve the problem, he raided the family toy chest and built two spooling towers on either side of his scanner out of Legos, one for doling out film and the other for uptake.

The bulk of the towers was constructed out of a rainbowed assemblage of regular Lego pieces while the hand-crank reels were comprised of vintage Lego Technics gears and axles. Simonson scanned the film letter by letter, turning the Technics gear to advance the film to the next frame. The longtime Lego fan even devised a clever Lego locking arm — it flopped down into the teeth of the gear when needed — to keep the film in tension while it was being scanned or cranked.

His makeshift Photo-Typositor got the job done, but Simonson speculated about automating the film-scanning process. "If I had the Lego Mindstorms system, which allows you to add motors, light sensors, etc., I could control the whole thing from my computer." Simonson's digital versions of Martin's Fotura and Bagatelle fonts should be out sometime early next year.

—*Jason Kottke*

≫ **Read Mark Simonson's description of his Lego mechanism at** *marksimonson.com/article/105/lego-the-type-designers-friend*.

Photograph by Mark Simonson

Eunicycle

If simplicity is the heart of elegance, then this one-wheeled motorized scooter far out-glams its two-wheeled cousins. **Trevor Blackwell's** self-built Eunicycle weighs in at less than 30 pounds, but can traverse a variety of surfaces — roads, sidewalks, and even grassy fields.

The Eunicycle self-balances by way of a feedback loop between a gyroscope and a motor perched just above its one wheel. When you tilt forward or backward, the wheel does, too, as it attempts to remain under the center of gravity.

Build it for about $1,500 in parts, including a microcontroller board, gyroscope, accelerometer, and other components. Perhaps the most important of these is a kill switch, allowing you to shut off the motor at the flick of a button. The maximum recommended speed of 12 miles an hour may not sound like the NASCAR definition of hauling ass, but when you're flailing through space on a single, motor-driven wheel — gravity isn't necessarily your friend.

—*Xeni Jardin*

≫ **A complete list of parts, the source code, and mechanical fabrication drawings are offered for free download at** tlb.org/eunicycle.html**.**

Jukebox Hero

Some people are just better prepared for an '80s revival. **Patrick Webb** has created a custom jukebox that screams garish authenticity and blasts out more than 700 of his favorites — including Poison, Mötley Crüe, and Bon Jovi.

The 38-year-old database manager started with the idea of having a digital repository for his CDs. He fastened together sheets of fiberboard and hauled a Pentium 133-Mhz computer and 15-inch monitor from the basement. Getting the PC to mimic a jukebox was easy, thanks to the well-known MAME software, or Multiple Arcade Machine Emulator.

The cabinet runs a free app called Arcade Jukebox 8, along with a dozen or so classic '80s games. He saw a photo of an old jukebox with what looked like tail lights, and bought a taxi light from a commercial fleet supplier, adding a coin-op device. "There's something funny about our teenager's friends coming over to stick quarters into it, but it makes that great 'clink!' sound."

—*Bob Parks*

≫ **Taxicab MAME:** *webbpage.net/jukebox*

Maker

OOZ and OZ »

By Dale Dougherty
Photography by
Emily Nathan

"We take in abandoned robotic dogs," says Natalie Jeremijenko.

She gets a warm laugh from a roomful of geeks at O'Reilly's Emerging Technology Conference (ETech) in San Diego this past March. Most people tire of their robotic dogs and end up selling them on eBay. "We need to rethink toys," she adds. "Most of

Maker

them are not truly engaging and have a very limited ability to teach us anything about the world we live in." Her idea is to "release" these domestic robots into the wild where, in the case of the Feral Robotics Project, hacked toy-dog robots can interact with each other and with humans as they sniff out contaminants in a landfill.

An Australian trained as an engineer, Jeremijenko recalls that her mother had the first microwave in Australia. "She believed that machines would one day do everything for us," says Jeremijenko, and immediately adds, "She was wrong." Jeremijenko taught in the Mechanical Engineering department at Yale, where she first began experimenting with robotic dogs.

Recently, Jeremijenko accepted a new appointment in the Visual Arts department at the University of California at San Diego (UCSD), where she is now teaching art students just enough electronics and programming to undertake her pet projects. These days, she sees herself moving between the worlds of engineering and art, just as she finds herself moving back and forth between New York and San Diego.

"I work on examining the cultural opportunities that technological innovations provide," she explains. She is particularly interested in the emerging field of social robotics. "I want to explore what's been left out of social robotics, which is more than having a handful of robots in a room. What does it mean to think of social robots, not just in terms of the robots, but in terms of the people too?"

Taunting Waterfowl and Talking with Fish

With the OOZ project, which is zoo spelled backwards and got its start in the Netherlands, Jeremijenko experimented with a robotic goose that can "play with, chase, and terrorize" other geese. In addition, the robotic goose can make goose sounds, and it will record and play back sounds made by other geese. It is possible to build a database of goose sounds, and humans can learn to communicate with geese through these interactions.

"Can we rescript our interactions with nature?" she asks. Instead of hunting geese, we can approach and talk to them (and likely annoy them). She says that this project is an example of using the open structure of participation, and that inter-

acting with a goose is much better than playing inside a closed system, such as a video game.

Another project allows people and fish to communicate. A board is placed in water with a hole above the waterline and a hole below the waterline. When a hand reaches inside the top hole, say to feed fish, the light goes on, telling fish that a human is there to feed them. When a fish passes through the lower hole, the light also goes on, letting a human know there is a fish wishing to be fed. "This shows you how technologies can be used to create an architecture of reciprocity," Jeremijenko remarks. The fish project was designed for a demonstration in Dublin, and she'd like to see it deployed in the Hudson River, the mention of which sends her on a riff.

> "We are forming an online distributed community which is interested in the low-cost adaptation of robotic dogs into activist instruments for exploring the local environment."

"We've designed an edible lure for fish. They can eat it and so can humans. Instead of hooks, the lure contains PCB-chelating agents, so we can do something good for the fish." She seems to take off in a different direction herself midstream. "Do you know where all the drugs we take end up? All the anti-depressants? They end up in the river. Can you imagine what's in the Hudson River? That's what we're doing to the fish and the frogs."

Jeremijenko's projects have more in common with performance art than with traditional science experiments. They are purposely designed to engage an audience and evoke a response. She invites the press to what she calls a "mediagenic" event so that she can reach this audience. Jeremijenko is only part wizard; the other part is pure Oz.

Robot School

On the day we caught up with Jeremijenko, she was planning to have her class release a pack of feral robotic dogs on the Mission Bay Landfill in San Diego. Local media, along with political figures, were invited.

As we trail along, Jeremijenko pops her head into the room designed as an art studio that serves as the student's shared lab space. "Will you be ready in five minutes?" she asks.

Nobody answers. The students' heads are focusing down on their robotic dogs, which suffer a variety of last-minute problems. Some students are soldering. Others are twisting wires. When Jeremijenko asks the same question again, the resounding reply is "No."

"We have to hurry," she urges them, knowing that there are people waiting at the landfill. Tristan Shone, the teaching assistant, shuttles from one group to the next trying to figure out which dogs are close to working and which are unsalvageable. Jeremijenko returns to her own office, which is filled with dozens of robotic dogs and a real white rabbit. "I feed her the same food I eat," she remarks.

The nine students work for about three to four weeks on the project after first locating their abandoned dogs. They consult web pages that tell them how to find dogs and upgrade them, based on instructions Jeremijenko created initially, and which have been improved upon by others and shared over the internet.

Student John Calmeyer wrote in the class wiki: "I went to Goodwill and bought one of the really ugly Dalmation Tekno dogs for $4.93. I was surprised to find out it even worked, which is to say that when I switched the on/off switch, it hobbled forward and wagged its lone remaining ear." Perversely, he named it "Kitty-Kitty."

Another student, Steven Chien, bought an i-Cybie for $55 on eBay, while Candice Storey took a trip home to adopt her little sister's Tekno. This Christmas present sat on the shelf for several years after her little sister "turned out to be a *live* cat person."

Jeff Miao bought a very furry dog known at Toys 'R' Us as the TIGER GOGO My Talkin' Pup and which sells for $30. He named it "Mia Mia." He had to perform major surgery on his dog, but before doing so, he writes that he "gently applied chloroform to sedate her before rolling her onto her back exposing her underbelly." He proceeded to remove the skin carefully before taking out various screws to create openings in the head and belly for new components.

How to Hack a Robot Dog

There are three basic upgrades. The first is to increase their range of motion. "This involves gently amputating the legs," Jeremijenko says, "and lowering the center of gravity, as well as widening the wheel base." A simple way to do that is to fit the robotic dog onto a chassis of a used RC car, as Chien's group did. The second upgrade is to give the dog a better brain. The class used the Cockroach II microcontroller and wrote some C code and then found a way to attach the logic board to the dog. The goal is to have the dog's brain follow its nose, which is the third upgrade, a nose that can sniff out environmental toxins. Each dog was outfitted with a sensor that measures the amount of solvent vapor in the air. Depending on the level of toxicity, the sensor will output a different voltage.

SNOOP DOGS: Jeremijenko's students release their hacked dogs at San Diego's Misson Bay Landfill.

1. Steven Chien makes a last minute adjustment on his feral robotic dog before letting it loose on a landfill in San Diego.

2. Best in Show! This hacked i-Cybie was the only feral robot dog to successfully sniff out the source of gas emanating from a pressurized tank.

3. John Calmeyer (left) and Jeff Miao (right) answer questions from television reporters covering the event.

4. Jeff Miao's furry robot gets off to a good start.

5. Dog chassis with hot wheels.

1.

2.

3.

4.

5.

Maker

From Orphan to Avenger

"We have to go NOW!" comes the professor's final instruction. The students begin placing their dogs and spare parts in laundry baskets, and rush out to their cars for a 20-minute drive to the Mission Bay Landfill.

On the way to the landfill, in the back of a van without seats, Jerejimenko explains that using toys "exploits the markets of scale for commercial toy production. This is the least expensive way to get your hands on corporate toys and rethink the corporate scripts of interaction."

She likes the i-Cybie, which she calls the "high end of the low end" for robotic dogs. She dislikes the Sony AIBO, saying that they are more expensive and not very interesting. The largest market for the Sony AIBO, she adds snidely, is engineering schools, which pay about $2,500 per pet, even with an academic discount.

> "Jeremijenko is only part wizard; the other part is pure Oz."

In addition to UCSD, there are feral robotic projects at Cornell University and in Dublin, London, San Francisco, and Brisbane, Australia.

"We are forming an online distributed community," explains Jeremijenko, "which is interested in the low-cost adaptation of robotic dogs into activist instruments for exploring the local environment."

Her goal is to release the dogs on sites of community interest such as Mission Bay. "This site was used by local military contractors," she adds, "where they dumped several thousand barrels in an unlined landfill right next to SeaWorld. It's at the former mouth of the San Diego River so there's a good deal of groundwater."

Who Let the Dogs Out?

When we arrive at the site, Jeremijenko is surprised by the number of video cameras and journalists. The landfill is also used as an airstrip for remote-controlled airplanes, and throughout the day these hobbyists seem irritated by the presence of both the dogs and the people. If

that wasn't annoying enough, the students are launching a large red balloon, which is outfitted with a rig to hold a video camera and is steered into position by ropes. The balloon-cam captures "a god's eye view" of the track.

At the release of the feral dog pack, only one of the five seems to actually work as expected. It's Mia Mia, the furry one, the one least likely to become feral. Others are experiencing fits before starting. The wheels spin, and soon, most of them are spreading out over the dirt.

Each dog's brain contains space-filling algorithms that describe how to cover the territory and what to do when they detect a toxic substance. Jeremijenko explains that since the dogs are programmed to respond to toxins, humans can learn by watching this response. It provides people with evidence. None of the dogs actually senses any sign of contaminants on the site. The release of a gas from a canister, used for testing, is discovered by Chien's i-Cybie robot. This dog circles back, following its nose, and runs into the canister and stops.

Later at ETech, Jeremijenko says, "By creating these dogs and releasing them as a pack, we create a mediagenic event that facilitates evidence-driven discussion. Because the dogs follow the concentration gradients, they display the information with their movements. Anyone from a 4-year-old to a grandmother can understand what the dogs are doing. With a site like this, we can have information that's unclear and there are many diverse, interested people. There might be an EPA report on the site or there might not be, and the report might be 15 years old or it might not be. Where does this information come from and how much of it is made public?"

Finally, she adds: "What happens when you change who has the evidence? You change the structure of participation between the expert audience and the lay audience. People can become the experts, and you know what? They are."

How much is that dogbot in the auction?
Student Ribecca Lee spent a considerable amount of time searching for the perfect used robot dog on eBay: "The dog must have qualities like flexibility in order to be effective."

Maker +HEIRLOOM TECHNOLOGY+

NICARAGUAN KNOW-HOW

By Tim Anderson

On a recent trip to Nicaragua, I saw a variety of homemade technologies. I met Juan Ramon (see photos at right) riding his front-wheel drive wheelchair in the town of Granada. He went zipping by in traffic. When I waved, he spun it around and zoomed up to talk to me.

It's a 5-speed, or 15-speed if he shifts the top chain-wheel by hand. The pedals have been replaced by handles. The back part is a regular wheelchair. The front part attaches just the same way the front caster assembly used to. This hand-pedal wheelchair is a great design solution. Not only does it allow him to get around as fast as a bicycle, but it's also great exercise. Many handicapped people in the U.S. have trouble getting enough exercise, and suffer higher rates of obesity and cardiovascular disease as a result. Here's an assortment of the other handmade technologies I saw.

I saw a lot of different kinds of bicycles modified with welding. There are plenty of rickshaw drivers here and every rickshaw is different. The lid on this bike's cargo box (pictured above) opens up to display the vendor's wares. And this bike (at left) uses casters from an office chair for a headset and has foot-operated front brakes.

Photography by Tim Anderson

+ PEOPLE MOVERS +

Used U.S. school buses are the main intercity transport. Getting around the country is a breeze. You just wave, and the bus stops and takes you in that direction for some absurdly low price. They weld up fancy cargo racks on top with ladders and luggage slides. Want to move your furniture or farm produce by bus? No problem. Fancy welding is super abundant in Nicaragua. East bloc countries were generous with welding equipment and training during the U.S. embargo. I think the tall exhaust stack in the back is required. It improves the air quality and keeps the buses quiet. The similar buses in Guatemala often have no exhaust system at all and sound like machine guns when they go up a steep hill.

I wish the U.S. had such a good, entrepreneurial transportation system. Once you get to town, there is a whole cornucopia of vehicle types to carry you around: trucks with benches and awnings, vans, old city buses from Brazil, etc. In addition to regular, private taxis, they have "collectivo" (shared) taxis that keep picking up more passengers headed the same direction until they're full, so it's cheap for everyone.

For about the same price, you can take a horse-drawn taxi — a car that runs on grass! The wheels are shod with strips from truck tires. Parts of the harness are made from strips cut from other parts of the tire. The horse collar is made from pieces of rerod bent to shape and covered with leather.

HAULIN' STUFF

Wooden wheelbarrows, like the one shown at right, are everywhere. The axle is made from rerod and the wooden wheels have treads from car tires nailed onto them. I thought they looked a bit crude, but the users seem to love them. The traditional farm wagon of the country is a larger version of these wheelbarrows.

If you need an instant wagon or bike trailer, try this: a wagon made with bicycle forks and wheels. Two bolts through the side of the fork hold it to the side of the box.

Wagons like this are the "contractor's pickup" in Granada, a colonial town on Lake Nicaragua. There's a lot of restoration work there, fueled by an influx of American retirees.

TOOLS

Here's a tool that's used like a blender (below). You put the big end in the drink and spin the handle between your hands. I met Marlene Monje, who mixes beverages with a wooden blender. The Nicaraguans seem to have more types of cold, non-alcoholic drinks than anyone else.

Nicaraguan Coffee Maker (at left). Every home and restaurant has one of these. You put the grounds in the flannel sock thing and pour the hot water through it into the coffeepot or cup underneath. There's a piece of wire in the rim of the "sock" to keep it from falling through the wire loop it rests on.

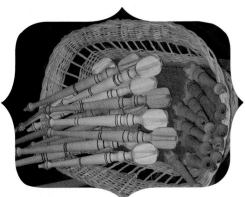

A cepillo de raspado is like a plane for making snow cones from a block of ice.

SHELTER

The colonial houses are mostly single-story, with courtyards, tile roofs, massive adobe walls, and very high ceilings. These features combine to make air conditioning unnecessary. They're really nice houses. In small towns, people leave their front doors open; in bigger towns, they have the grillwork closed and the door open. It's a pleasure to walk down the street in the evening and pass the domestic scenes revealed in each lighted parlor.

You can build such a house from not much more than dirt, grass, and sticks. Many houses have quite a lot of wooden structure embedded in the adobe. This probably enables them to withstand earthquakes better. That's important in a country with such active geology.

Houses often have a lot of fibrous material, like straw, mixed in the bricks. I saw no signs of decay in the fibers or wooden beams buried in the walls.

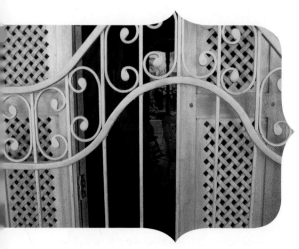

This church in Leon (above, right) was destroyed during the fighting to take a prison across the street. They left it this way as a monument, and built a brand new church right next to it. Also, the old prison (below, right) now contains a folklore museum full of stuffed figurines representing characters from folktales.

✛ THINGS OF THE PAST ✛

Churches seem to use plain, adobe bricks without straw, but with cement or brick around the doors and windows. In a building that's being used, there's no way to tell what's in the walls because they're plastered and painted over. There's an old convent in Granada that's been converted to a museum. The restorers left bare patches so you could see what's inside the wall — the buried beams, patched many times after each attack by marauders or what-have-you. Also in evidence are broken roof tiles, adobe blocks made with straw or horsehair, plain mud bricks, lath, reeds. Over the years they've used just about everything to build adobe buildings.

Antique water filter (pictured above). The upper vessel is a thick bowl carved from porous volcanic rock. The water filters through and drips into the lower pot. The whole thing stands about waist high. I saw this at the Moyogalpa Museum, Isla Ometepe, in Lake Nicaragua.

Caltrops in the Gallery of Heroes and Martyrs in Masaya. Here's a welded version of an ancient

weapon. Sandinistas put them on roads to delay army vehicles in the revolution against Somoza. This museum is mostly devoted to photos of people who died in the Revolution.

The Next Whole Earth Catalog has a good section reviewing books about how to build adobe buildings. The catalog is a great way to get a sense of the scope of traditional and "alternative" technologies. It's 25 years old now, but the good thing about traditional techniques is they never go out of date.

(ISBN:0394739515) Brand, Stewart (editor) New York, New York, U.S.A.: Point/Random House, 1980. Paperback. Folio 15" tall. 608p. index illus.

The islanders used to bury their dead in these ceramic urns shaped like a pregnant woman's belly (shown above). The symbol on the large jar is a bat, whose spirit helps the dead see their way. The family that owns the museum has always lived in Moyogalpa. Possibly, they are descended from the people once buried in these jars. Not exactly how-to hobbyist tech, but they're such beautiful, poetic objects I thought you should see them.

Maker

BLOCKHEADS

Lego: The ultimate prototyping material. Seriously. By Bob Parks

Adrian Marshall decided that he'd need a very convincing scale model to sell his latest idea. The British designer of factory robots was to meet the board of directors of a large food company, who wanted an industrial robot that could move ten arms independently and burn a picture of the Rugrats cartoon characters on pancakes randomly placed around a moving skillet. It had to be done in under 0.8 seconds in a hot industrial kitchen. Of course, he used the only prototyping material suitable for such a tough job: Lego.

"I always use Lego to present to customers," says Marshall. "If it's simple enough to be made from Lego, then the scaled-up version will be robust enough to survive in the field."

It may be ironic that a toy may be the greatest prototyping medium ever invented, but since the arrival of the primary-colored plastic blocks in 1949, engineers have used them to envision new products. And with the advance of Lego Technic in the late 1970s, inventors could spec out more complicated machines with wheels, gears, and motors.

"Technic is coming from the engineer's mindset," says Hayes Raffle, a researcher using Lego to develop modular robot toys at MIT's Media Lab. "You can replicate the movement you find in motors and other mechanical linkages quickly and cheaply." Now, dozens of university programs across the country supply Lego Technic for students to design everything from unmanned military vehicles to laser-surgery devices.

Part of the Lego prototype popularity may be that everyone seems to have a cache of blocks in a closet somewhere. That's certainly the case with Tim Abbot, an Indiana-based entrepreneur, who used a Dremel tool to cut small holes in his son's blocks and built an innovative backyard sprinkler system. Abbot's Hydro-Edge will be sold nationally this summer. Or how about Kevin Mackie, from Scotland, who used Lego to build a prototype new drum pedal? The design is now used by musicians including Iron Maiden, Chick Corea, and James Brown.

Sooner or later, however, Legos run out. Factory roboticist Marshall says he often finds himself in a crunch for specific pieces, so he orders large batches from educational distributors online. Seekers of rare parts must look to eBay, trade among Lego enthusiasts online, or participate in closed auctions listed in newsgroups and Lego builder's sites like lugnet.com.

Lego has some inherent limitations as well. While some builders pride themselves on using only what's in the catalog — Chicago's Jonathan Brown created a Rubik's Cube solver and Lego juggler using only virgin bricks — even Brown concedes: "[Legos have] lousy strength-to-weight characteristics. They're great for small models, but not so good for large models."

In making factory prototypes, Marshall reinforces his structures with side plates of medium-density fiberboard, aluminum, or steel. "Fine adjustments to geometry aren't easy," he notes.

To make Lego creations more rugged, MIT's Raffle uses hot glue. Meanwhile, professional Lego sculptor Eric Harshbarger swears by Oatey All-Purpose Cement. (He once used seven pounds of the stuff to build a full-size office desk as part of a commission.)

Adjustments to size work best using the carbide cutting wheel on a Dremel; with flat plates, the experts suggest lightly scoring an X-Acto knife along a steel ruler and then making deeper subsequent cuts.

In the end, Marshall's client was blown away by his pancake-stamping machine and ordered a full-sized version in stainless steel to the tune of $200,000. He used a stereolithography machine to make custom parts for a second prototype and recreated the design virtually in 3D Studio, a CAD software program. (Other Lego builders hone their creations using LDraw, a free CAD software made especially for Lego parts.) The toy may not be the best option for going into production, but it's great for delivering a proof of concept.

Bob Parks (bobparks@yahoo.com) lives in Vermont, where he contributes to Wired, Business 2.0, and other magazines.

Photo illustration by Kirk von Rohr
Legos from the private collections of Kindy Connally Stewart and Branden von Rohr

Maker

MAKER FAIR

By Arwen O'Reilly

Everyone at the Maker Fair at O'Reilly's ETech Conference in San Diego this March seemed to be having a blast. It can't just have been the beer and wine, though, because people stuck around for the entire three hours. Set up like a grade school science fair, 12 *Makers* manned stations around the room to explain their projects, and hundreds of tech enthusiasts crowded around. Disturbed only by a marshmallow shooter showdown between Tim O'Reilly and Jeff Bezos, energy and attention were high. People learned to solder, restore vintage amps, and hack everything in sight. In the end, though, the real proof of the evening's success was the fact that, unlike almost every other conference social event, the food tables were all but forgotten.

Photography by Emily Nathan

Dale Dougherty

GOOGLE
DIY PATTERNS

GOOGLE REMADE THE WEB WITH A NEW KIND OF LANGUAGE FOR GETTING WHAT WE WANT FROM A WEB BROWSER.

I SELDOM TYPE URLS ANYMORE. I USE THE Google search window in the Firefox browser.

Think about how this change reduces the value of domain names. When we decided on the name MAKE for our magazine, we looked for the obvious domain name, which was taken but not in use. Not to worry. Makezine.com was a suitable alternative, and as of early March, when I type "make" into Google, our website shows up third on the list. Add the word "magazine" and it's first. Having a killer domain name doesn't matter the way it used to.

The Domain Name System provides a static binding address, like when you provide a street address to

> "Google is like a fast-food restaurant offering a limited menu. The goal is to get you in and out as quickly as possible."

someone who asks you where you live. Google provides a dynamic binding that changes based on the experience of users, more like the question you're asked when you answer your cellphone: where are you now?

Google is proving as adept at marrying great engineering and great design as Apple and Sony. The Google search engine is a second-generation web application that reflects new insights on the web, based on experience that wasn't available to first-generation applications.

Amazon, the gold standard of the first generation,

is like a department store with lots of floors and lots of choices. Google is like a fast-food restaurant offering a limited menu. The goal is to get you in and out as quickly as possible. Yahoo practically invented the portal concept with a collection of services all tied together. Google came along and got rid of the clutter. It's the anti-portal. Now they are redesigning standalone services, such as email and mapping, that are fresh and fascinating.

Design is a creative process that continually re-examines our experiences and recognizes the patterns that emerge from new and old ideas. Architect Christopher Alexander wrote a famous series of books in which he sought to recover the patterns that are inherent in buildings. He considered patterns to be rules of thumb. Every barn shares many of the same patterns, but each barn can be unique.

In *A Pattern Language* (1977), Alexander explains that a "pattern describes a problem which occurs over and over again in our environment, and then describes the core of the solution to the problem, in such a way that you can use this solution a million times over, without ever doing it the same way twice." Alexander's ideas were then picked up by Erich Gamma, et al. They then applied them to software construction in the book *Design Patterns* (1995).

A DIY project is a design challenge which can be described as a set of patterns. In MAKE, we want to develop a pattern language that helps our readers build on the ideas and insight of others who hack, tweak, and tinker. In this way, you can make technology solve your own problems, but you aren't doing it completely on your own.

Dale Dougherty is the editor and publisher of MAKE. He can be reached at dale@oreilly.com.

Maker

RECYCLED RUBBER

It's more fun to make a laptop bag from an old wetsuit than it is to buy one. By Saul Griffith

It's easy to make money, as long as that's all you wish to do. I find it easier to make things than to make money, and it appears that that's all I do. Fortunately we live in a society where many raw materials are free as long as you have a few favorite dumpsters.

The false economies of making your own stuff are addictive. Most everything I own is an amalgam of trash reconfigured with a rather large and expensive set of scratched and greasy tools. It's always a good idea at the time: make a bicycle trailer (the store-bought ones don't suit my needs), build a kite, sew a laptop bag.

Jack O'Neill was probably in a similar situation when the surfing boom of the 1950s saw many Southern Californians enjoying a new lifestyle of longboards and Woodies. He, however, was stuck in San Francisco, as I am, where year-round water temperatures hover in the 50s (Fahrenheit). Not to be stopped cold in feeding his addiction of surfing, Jack set about pioneering the wetsuit.

Like most backyard innovators, he started with that glorious jumble of the local surplus store and its army/navy frogmen suits. Surfing was still small enough that most people knew most other people, and everyone was hacking their gear to get more out of their passion. One contemporary of Jack's was known for wearing a navy jumper soaked in Thompson's water seal — better than coating yourself in a thick layer of pig fat, but not the convenience they all yearned for.

The frogmen suits were pieces of rubber glued together that — along with a layer of air trapped in your underwear — would provide some insulation,

though rough surf always found a way to open everything up and throw cold water on your ideas and other sensitive body parts.

Jack's first wetsuit was polyvinylchloride (PVC) glued to thin sheets of plastic in the form of a vest. It was hard to work with, somewhat fragile, and wore out quickly.

Like most lifestyle surfers, odd jobs were the order of the day and "Eureka!" came to Jack while he was carpeting the aisles of a DC-3 passenger aircraft. Under the carpet was neoprene. It was used on planes as sound and thermal insulation. It is easy to bond, floats, and is flexible and robust.

Neoprene is a closed-cell foam. Closed-cell foams are basically thousands of tiny bubbles surrounded by rubber where none of the bubbles join any others, making it waterproof. Open-cell foams are those where all the bubbles intersect and overlap. These become waterlogged and don't trap air, which is a better insulator than any plastic or rubber by itself.

Jack starting making wetsuits out of neoprene and an industry was born. Wetsuits have changed enormously since the 1950s with new designs, more supple materials and stretch zones, new stitches patterns, and new glues to eliminate stitching altogether.

Anyway, all of this is to say I just bought a new laptop, one of those cultish ones with the piece of fruit on the cover. It's the first laptop I ever bought, because I've generally been able to convince the military-industrial-education complex to buy them for me. Fortunately, they never seemed to mind that a laptop has a six-month life expectancy in the hands of a lifestyle surfer and cyclist. It's a good idea

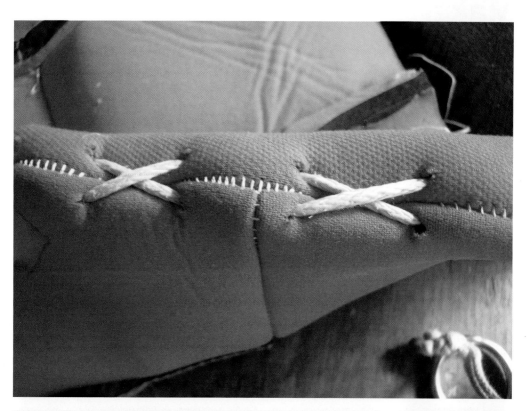

to land on your laptop when you crash your bicycle; it's softer than your spine and, despite thoughts to the contrary, is less valuable than your collarbone.

However, now I have to pay for laptops myself, so I thought I'd try and make it last at least a year or two. Browsing the laptop bag offerings at the store, they

Neoprene can be hand-stitched, which creates a wonderful Frankenstein aesthetic.

seemed to offer far too little padding for my liking, and all looked like an advertisement for laptop theft. I had some old wetsuits — the kind with tears in all the wrong places, which prevent you from being able to pee inside the wetsuit to keep yourself warm. (Admit it, you do it too.)

HOW TO MAKE A LAPTOP BAG

Wash and deodorize the wetsuit. Gentle detergents, a dash of vinegar, and warm-water hand agitation does the trick nicely.

Wetsuits don't have a lot of flat straight pieces, so you'll see mine is made from strips cut from the least worn pieces of the old suit. I don't have much need for measuring — I just eyeballed and oversized the panels a little to allow for the seams and ended up with a stretchy case, like sexy spandex for your computer.

Neoprene can be hand-stitched, which gives a wonderful Frankenstein aesthetic, but it's a lot faster to use a sewing machine, and you'll be able to make more mistakes without feeling guilty about starting over. Most strong home sewing machines will do the trick; just make sure you use a large denim needle and thick polyester thread. I have sailmaker's Dacron thread, which is perfect.

If your machine is weak, you may need to manually help the poor little motor by winding with the machine on the down-stroke and letting it find it's own way home coming back up. This is slow, but better than hand stitching. If the neoprene is really thick, you'll get better results by lifting the sewing machine's foot completely to accommodate your wad of material.

I put my seams on the outside. I'd like to say this was to make it look cool (which I think it does) but it was really because I forgot to turn it inside out before I was done. When I finished sewing the thing, I realized the bag needed pockets for batteries, power packs, passports, and a toothbrush. So I placed a couple of squares of neoprene on the inside. Because it is stretchy, it's pretty tolerant of low accuracy. I reinforced the sides with old polyester hiking bootlaces. When tied in a loop, they fastened perfectly to the shoulder strap I found on some old luggage that had been offered to the gods on the side of the road. To clip it all together I used a couple of child-restraint belts scavenged from abandoned shopping carts. Apparently, it's illegal to use parts from abandoned shopping carts.

The result is lush, soft, bouncy, waterproof, and orange. All things I like, plus it will stretch to fit two notebooks and a burrito. I got overzealous and even built a matching iPod case that has protected my music machine in dozens of falls.

While I don't think it's sufficiently wonderful to start my own O'Neill-type business, it is a fun bag, gets noticed (by hipsters not thieves), and makes me feel like I foiled the landfill again. All that, and it only took about four hours to make.

This article also took about four hours to write and paid me enough to buy several laptop bags. False economies indeed, but I'd wrestle the auto-threading mechanism happily to do it all again.

Saul Griffith thinks about open source hardware while working with the power-nerds at Squid Labs (*www.squid-labs.com*).

Scoring Used Neoprene

If you don't surf or dive, ask a buddy who does. He or she should be able to set you up with a thrashed suit.

You can recycle some of the 5 billion dot.com mousepads that still plague us — they're made of neoprene, too.

On eBay, you'll find plenty of wetsuits being sold by people who liked the idea of surfing after watching *Endless Summer* and gave up after swallowing a pint of ocean the first time they got in the water.

You can also buy new 51"x83" sheets of neoprene from places like foamorder.com, but that sort of defeats the purpose.

THE CODE DA VINCI LIVED BY

Renaissance hacks by the father of all geeks.

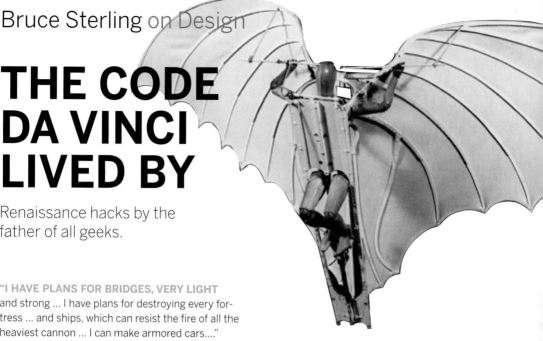

Leonardo dissected bats and birds to design the wings for his human-powered flying machines.

"I HAVE PLANS FOR BRIDGES, VERY LIGHT and strong ... I have plans for destroying every fortress ... and ships, which can resist the fire of all the heaviest cannon ... I can make armored cars...."

That's Leonardo da Vinci, asking the Duke of Milan for a job, ten years before Columbus discovered America.

Leonardo got that job. He went to Milan to make huge bronze statues, giant cathedrals, enormous canals, secret tunnels, and a bristling host of giant, terrifying, remarkably sadistic war machines. Leonardo had plenty of plans — volumes full of them, plans stuffed in the margins of his plans. But Leonardo never shipped the products. He never made any of those things.

In practice, Leonardo mostly made ingenious special effects for festival entertainments. His glamorous stage shows for dukes and kings were the main reason these worthies kept him around. Leonardo also painted masterpieces, but reluctantly and not very many. Nowadays his paintings are what's left to us to see. The royal festival entertainments vanished like soap bubbles, as soon as his amazed contemporaries stopped saying, "Wow!"

As for his glorious cities, super-machines, and giant canals ... some were possible, barely. But making them required an aggressive, full-scale engineering outfit like General Dynamics or Halliburton, not a visionary wizard in a velvet hat. The Renaissance couldn't work that way, because no mere king or duke could give Leonardo a budget that size, or that many resources in men and materials. His ideas were glorious — too glorious to have a business model.

"Wow" is the unifying theme that runs through the great man's scatterbrained interests in anatomy, human flight, submarines, mathematics, physics, and hydrodynamics. Leonardo sketched tens of thousands of fantasy machines, from ball bearings to gigantic cranes, yet somehow, they always stay on one message: "Leonardo is amazing." His notebooks are an endless series of air-guitar solos in a world that hasn't yet invented orchestras.

Leonardo's a one-man show. When Leonardo envisions a super-cannon, it's a multi-barreled blunderbuss that one guy can use to destroy an army. When he imagines an airplane, it's one guy soaring on batwings. His submarine is one guy secretly drowning an entire ship full of enemies. When his giant war chariot chops a company of soldiers like wheat in a combine harvester, you just know that the victims will be forced to wonder, "Who the heck did this to us? He must be some kind a genius!"

A dredge is a machine for digging with a big scoop. Most of us would consider a dredge to be a very practical, roughneck, and muddy kind of machine. A Leonardo dredge is not just a big shovel with pulleys. It's a splendid altar to canal digging, a showy, towering enterprise whose nifty gearings must attract public attention for miles around. Canals are supposed to be handy waterways where people can ship stuff in boats. Leonardo's canals, extensively planned but never built, are Leonardo's personal adornments to the map of Italy, a kind of environmental art installation.

When Leonardo explores human anatomy, healing other people is the last thing on his mind. It's

Model from a sketch by Leonardo da Vinci: The Inventions of Leonardo da Vinci was donated to The Exhibition Alliance by the IBM Corporation. The exhibition is circulated by The Exhibition Alliance Inc., Hamilton, NY.

all about his need to figure out how human flesh works; it's got nothing to do with him trying to cure people or give them any kind of benefit. Even his dead cadavers seem surprised and impressed by him: "Wow! Look! Leonardo cut me open and learned my anatomical secrets!" In his autopsy

> Leonardo sketched tens of thousands of fantasy machines, from ball-bearings to gigantic cranes, yet somehow, they always stay on one message: "Leonardo is amazing."

work, Leonardo radiates hackerly glee at having pulled off a scary, little-known, semi-legal, very difficult stunt.

Leonardo is always particularly eager to do amazing things that any normal guy would consider impossible. So quite a few of his coolest inventions really are impossible. It's not that Leonardo is ever a fraud — for instance, he manages to figure out, from his own researches, that perpetual motion is a swindle. That's a genuine tribute to his common sense. But the science of physics hasn't been invented yet, so Leonardo has no way to calculate how much energy his imaginary machines require to run.

Leonardo sketches out ingenious systems of worm gears, cranks, and ratchets — spinning wheels, counterweights, giant timber beams — but where's the engine? In Leonardo's world the "engine" is usually a solo guy. He's the ideal Leonardo engine worker, and when Leonardo sketches him out, he's commonly this tiny little guy in the corner — half-naked, firmly muscled, and really getting into his labors.

He looks pretty much like Charlie Chaplin trapped by machinery in *Modern Times*, but full of Renaissance. When it comes to a really tough job, like flying, Leonardo will put four guys on the job. Leonardo's helicopter has four guys running around pushing capstans and driving a big paper screw up into the air. In reality, those four guys would have to be four 200-horsepower aircraft engines.

What Leonardo needed, to make his dreams leave paper and take flight, was the Industrial Revolution. He never got one, because that was centuries away.

What Leonardo's fate was to become was what he had most wanted to be, all along — Leonardo from Vinci, an Officially Amazing Guy. He finally died, much respected and pampered, in the entourage of the King of France. The King never asked Leonardo to do anything much or carry out any practical assignment. It was more than enough for the King just to listen to Leonardo ranting about the amazing stuff he'd figured out.

Leonardo was blazingly eager to do incredible things, using secret techniques he had learned himself, demonstrated in as public and showy a way as possible. For Leonardo, that's what technology was all about. So he was an engineer. And mostly an artist. But above all, an ego-driven, visionary entrepreneur. Bill Gates owns his codices. Leonardo da Vinci was the father of the modern geek.

In his Codex Atlanticus, Leonardo stated about his parachute: "Anyone can jump from no matter what height without any risk whatsoever."

Bruce Sterling (bruce@well.com) is a science fiction writer and part-time design professor.

HDTV
ON YOUR MAC

Watch and record high definition television with a $10 antenna, a $175 decoder card, and some free software. By Erica Sadun

The other night, I popped over to Target to pick up an antenna. You remember what those are, don't you? Those telescoping metallic things that connect to television sets? That predate cable? Rabbit ears? I was about to buy my first antenna in something like 20 years. I am such a cable-generation baby, I felt like I was walking into a time warp (and not the good Rocky Horror kind, either) until I walked into the actual aisle.

It was the packaging that hit me first. Target had about a dozen or so antennas on sale, and every single one (and let me repeat that, just to be emphatic, Every Single One) had an HDTV digital-ready sticker on it. I hadn't walked back into the past — I had just entered the present. This was the world of Terrestrial HDTV: high-definition television broadcast over the airwaves.

The GE "Futura" unit I picked up (got to laugh at the name, but it was only ten bucks) proclaimed that it was "designed to receive the highest quality broadcast HDTV signal." You've just got to love that.

As a platform, Macintosh is a little late to the HDTV party. PC solutions (both Windows and Linux) are more abundant and better supported, and if you use these systems, you can visit copperbox.com and eff.org/broadcastflag to find out how to make

WARNING: BROADCAST FLAG APPROACHING

If you're reading this after July 1, 2005, then it's too late. You won't be able to buy an HDTV tuner that can record programs in high-resolution format.

July 1 is the date the FCC will begin enforcing its "Broadcast Flag" mandate, which requires manufacturers of digital television tuners (including PC tuner cards) to include so-called "content protection" in their hardware. That means DTV tuners made after this date must be able to detect and honor a content flag that makes it impossible to record HDTV in full-resolution. Worse, content that has been flagged can only be saved on systems that support "digital rights management" technology, which means programs can't be copied to other players. In other words, forget about burning *Alias* to DVD so you can watch it on your portable player. The Broadcast Flag makes it so you can't.

However, if you build or buy an HDTV player or recorder before July 1, you'll be able to enjoy a full-featured system without restrictions on your rights to time-shift and space-shift content. So get cracking. *—Mark Frauenfelder*

(For more information about the Broadcast Flag, visit the websites listed at left.)

a non-Mac HDTV viewer/recorder. Sticking with Mac, you can either fork over the medium-to-big bucks to buy a turnkey solution, like Elgato's EyeTV 500 ($350 USD) (oreilly.com/go/eyetv), or you can try to put together your own system using a decoder card, an antenna, some freeware software, and a lot of love, elbow grease, and spit. Naturally, I chose the latter.

HDTV Broadcasts

Author's note: This article discusses American NTSC broadcast of high-definition television. Apologies to readers from other countries.

When you watch TV on a traditional television set, you're watching fairly low-quality video. The analog signal contains 525 vertical scan lines with a horizontal resolution of, say, 400 to 500 dots. And of that whole picture, you can see maybe two-thirds of it because your good old picture-tube-based television set does something called "overscanning" to protect the picture tubes against the effects of aging. Enter something called ATSC (atsc.org). ATSC stands for Advanced Television Systems Committee, an American standards body that defined a way to transmit pure digital signals using MPEG-2 compression to your television set. (Yes, that's the same MPEG-2 compression used by DVDs.)

When you watch TV on a traditional analog set, the television (or a converter box) grabs this digital signal, converts it to analog format, and displays it. It may look better than the quality you're used to, but it's nowhere near as good as the quality you'd see on a purely digital set. Analog TVs can't even begin to do justice to HDTV's 720 or even 1080 broadcast lines of resolution, let alone the horizontal resolution of 1280 or 1920 dots per line.

Finding a Broadcast

To find digital broadcasts in your area, point your browser to Antenna Web (antennaweb.org). You'll need to enter your zip code to perform the search.

To start, click Submit after entering your zip code. A new page opens, displaying all the over-the-air broadcasts in your vicinity. Click the Show Digital Stations Only radio button. This limits the display to digital broadcasts.

Step 1: Get Started

In order to start watching HDTV on your Mac, you need to have a certain number of items on hand. These include the following:

 A higher-end Mac. You'll need a dual 1GHz Mac or a single 1.44GHz Mac at a minimum. Even faster is even better. HDTV takes up a lot of processing speed. Also make sure you have lots and lots of free disk space, so you can record your programs as you watch them. You'll need to use a tower-type system with at least one open PCI slot.

A DVICO Fusion HDTV 3 Gold ATSC card. I picked one up for about $175, shipped from Copperbox (copperbox.com). The DVICO website (oreilly.com/go/dvico) lists several vendors.

Tip: Want to save a couple of bucks at Copperbox? If you have a spare opossum picture (even road kill), email it to patrick@copperbox.com to claim your discount. My brother-in-law once gave me a set of 'possum coasters, complete with tire tracks. Finally, they (and my handy-dandy flatbed scanner) came in useful for something!

An antenna. Target. $10, give or take.

It's easy to get set up. Just crack open your Mac case and install the PCI card. Close the case back up, connect your antenna to the card and you're set. You'll need to install a driver and the proper viewing software, as you'll see in the next section.

Step 2: Download the Software

You can find most of the software you'll need at John Dalgliesh's defyne.org/dvb/ website. John is the author of iTele, tunetest, and more. (He is also a kind and patient man, who helpfully answered many technical questions for me.) Here's a list of the software you'll want to have on hand.

The MMInputFamily Device Drivers. In order to view HDTV, you'll need to install these device drivers so your software can communicate properly with your capture card. Download directly at oreilly.com/go/MMInput.

iTele, a viewing application that lets you watch your HDTV programs. iTele automatically scans the airwaves for active signals, display them for you to watch, and record them to disk. It's currently at version 0.5.7. Download directly at oreilly.com/go/itele.

Types of Digital Video Broadcasts

In the United States, you can receive any of three kinds of digital video broadcasts. These include:

✳ Terrestrial digital video, which is broadcast over the airways using the ATSC standard. Your local network affiliates and public television stations send out the signal from their local towers. This makes the signals directional, so some antenna adjustment may be needed to properly receive the broadcast.

✳ Satellite digital video, which is broadcast via satellite television using a variety of standards, many of which are proprietary. Some satellite companies (like DIRECTV and Dish) also provide terrestrial ATSC tuners to their customers to receive local network broadcasts.

✳ Cable digital video is broadcast over cable systems that provide digital TV service. HDTV channels are added as they are established, usually in the upper reaches of the numbering system. As with satellite broadcasts, cable providers use a number of standards including OpenCable and DVB-C.

From a Mac point of view, reception options are limited. Elgato's EyeTV 500 can receive, display, and record both terrestrial and (some) cable signals. U.S. do-it-yourselfers can receive terrestrial ATSC signals and unencoded Open-Cable transmissions. (Unfortunately, few cable companies transmit unencrypted HDTV.)

✳ **Mplayer** is a port of the Linux movie-viewing application. iTele supports two ways of watching video. You can use an internal viewer (that is to say, within the iTele program itself) or Mplayer as an external viewer. Download your copy of the OS X MPlayer from SourceForge. The current version is 2b8r4, available at mplayerosx.sourceforge.net.

Step 3: Test Your Card

After installing the software applications and drivers, it's time to give the card a spin and start watching HDTV. In the following steps, you'll learn how to use iTele to watch and to record HDTV broadcasts.

1. Launch iTele. As this is your first time running the program, it will not yet know which broadcast channels it can receive.

2. Adjust your antenna, pointing it towards the greatest density of broadcast signals in your area.

3. Open the Inputs window (Window -> Inputs, Command-1). Here's where you need to hold your breath. If you see your card listed, then everything's OK. If not, then it's time to make sure you've installed the drivers and maybe to open up your Mac again and see if you've installed the board correctly.

4. Select the DVICO Fusion card by clicking on its name in the Inputs window. As you do so, a drawer will open at the bottom of the window, which shows further details (or it will in future releases of iTele).

5. Click the Scan button in the drawer to begin scanning the airwaves for digital broadcasts.

6. Enter a location after you've been prompted. Choose Korea and North America and click Scan.

7. Wait. It takes several minutes for the scanning process to proceed. The Channels window shows the progress of the search. Do not be alarmed if iTele only finds one or two broadcasts. Remember, they are directional.

Step 4: Watch

After scanning has finished, the remaining channels listed in the Channels Window (Window -> Channels, Command-2) are what you can watch. The Channel menu is a little tricky, so here's a quick overview before you continue.

✳ **Channel -> Watch and Channel -> Watch Off:** These two menu items turn "watching" (versus recording or anything else) on and off. It's a little counterintuitive, but it does work.

> "You could spend a lot of money buying a digital HDTV set, or you could arrange to watch things on your computer for a lot less money."

✳ Channel -> Record On and Channel -> Record Off: Same idea, but for recording.

✳ Channel -> Watch Full Screen and Channel -> Watch Little: This pair of menu items controls whether you watch a full-resolution display (even bigger than your screen resolution!) or a smaller-resolution display.

✳ Channel -> Use Internal Display: Leave this menu item unchecked to watch in MPlayer. I recommend proceeding in the following fashion:

1. Select the Channel you want to watch in the Channels window.

2. Choose Channel -> Record Off. Make sure you don't record until you're ready to do so.

3. Choose Channel -> Watch Little. A small screen is easier to watch at first.

4. Wait as iTele launches MPlayer and starts displaying your video.

Step 5: Record

Recording HDTV couldn't be easier. When you're ready to start recording, choose Channel -> Record On. You don't even have to be watching at the time. iTele starts capturing the already-compressed MPEG-2 signal and saves it to your home folder. After it finishes recording (Channel -> Record Off), you can watch the file by opening it and playing it back in MPlayer. Just remember, the file will be big!

Final Thoughts

So, if you're not quite ready to jump into the HDTV waters with both feet, this approach should serve you well while you watch how things shake out. You can also use this article as a way to rationalize that 23-inch Apple Cinema Display you've been yearning for. The approach could be something like this: "But look at all the money I saved by not buying a High Def TV!"

Reprinted with permission from MacDevCenter.com.

Erica Sadun has written, co-written, and contributed to almost two dozen books about technology.

A MAKER STORY

Termite Insurance Extra

The "Legnatile" is a Compaq Armada 700, running Linux, and covered with a wooden shell that has been "totally handcrafted using ancient methods." Almost every square inch of the surface of the laptop, down to its hinges, is covered in varnished hardwood. Its creator, Mr. Zaverio from Italy, sells them on eBay for about 1,000 euros each. For more photos, see: zaverio.net/laptop/legnatile/index-en.html

Make:Projects

r Geheimkurier

die

Die Unterwasser
Bestien

AUTO
GAME

RENTACOM
Game Action

ITT FAMILY GAMES 554-33 391

Meteor Defense

PIGS IN SPACE/E.T.
ROBOT TANK/PRESSURE COOKIER

RETRO GAME HEAVEN: THE ATARI 2600PC

By Joe Grand

After fitting a full-featured wireless PC system into an old Atari 2600 case, you can watch movies, surf the web, and play hundreds of retro games. >>

Set up: p.54   **Make it:** p.56   **Use it:** p.84

UPGRADING NOSTALGIA WITH THE ATARI 2600PC

I'm a historian of retro videogame systems and enjoy playing games on many different systems. I have a personal connection to the Atari 2600, which is probably related to my nostalgia for growing up with one. From an engineering perspective, the design of the Atari 2600 hardware is both simple and complex — yin and yang, so to speak — and it has enticed me for many years.

The goal of this project is to cram a full-featured PC system into a retro Atari 2600 videogame case. Not only is this a real challenge, but it's extremely rewarding. Since I want to retain as much of the original look and feel of the Atari system as I can, I will be using part of the original Atari circuitry and the original game controllers. Also, the Atari 2600PC lets you play DVDs (and CDs) on your TV.

Joe Grand (joe@grandideastudio.com) is the president and principal electrical engineer of Grand Idea Studio, Inc., a product development and intellectual property licensing firm. He specializes in the invention and design of consumer electronics, toys, and video game technologies. His latest creations include the Parallax RFID Reader Module, the Gamecaster Cybercam, and the Stelladaptor Atari 2600 Controller-to-USB Interface.

1. Prepare the Case. Open the Atari 2600. Remove the circuitry. Wash case.

MAKING THE ATARI 2600PC

In order to convert an old Atari 2600 console into a PC that can play hundreds of retro video games and play DVD movies, you have to remove the guts and replace them with three components: a mini PC, a DVD drive, and some special adapters that let you use the original Atari controllers. Here's a summary of the steps.

2. Configure Components. Modify 2600 control panel, controller-to-USB interface, power supply, PC motherboard, and 2600 housing.

3. Add Components. Install DVD drive, controller adapters, PC motherboard, control panel, and power supply.

4. Finishing Up. Close case. Plug in. Install software. Play!

Illustration by Nik Schulz/L-Dopa.com

SET UP.

For this project, we need to purchase lots of pieces, which requires a substantial commitment of funding. On completion, the total financial damage for my particular configuration of Atari 2600PC case modification was a little over $700. Also, prepare to spend a significant amount of time fabricating and hacking components to get them to fit in the case. Basic soldering and desoldering skills are necessary (See MAKE, Volume 01 for a primer on soldering and desoldering).

Even though these lists of materials and tools seem rather specific, all the items are quite common and can easily be found online or at your local computer store. The actual speeds and capacities of the computer components are a personal preference; I chose midrange parts so my new PC wouldn't quickly become obsolete.

Make sure the components you purchase actually fit inside your enclosure. If possible, obtain the dimensions of each part, such as the motherboard, power supply, and hard drive. You can get the dimensions from manufacturer data sheets or product review pages. VIA Technologies (www.via.com.tw) makes a number of small, fully integrated PC motherboards based around the popular Mini-ITX form factor. The EPIA Nehemiah M10000 motherboard measures only 17cm by 17cm (6.7 inches per side) and packs all necessary peripherals into one single unit.

MATERIALS:

Atari VCS model CX2600A Four-switch woodgrain version

VIA Technologies EPIA Nehemiah M10000 [B] includes USB/FireWire backplane **[O]** and ATA133 hard drive cable. Available in computer stores and online from places such as *accupc.com, linitx.com,* and *mini-itx.com*

PC2100 DRAM [C] Micron DDR 512MB, 266MHz, 184-pin

2.5-inch laptop hard drive [D] Fujitsu MHS2060AT, 60GB

40-pin to 44-pin 2.5-inch laptop IDE hard drive cable adapter [A] For connecting a 2.5-inch laptop hard drive to standard PC motherboard connectors

Slim CD-RW/DVD combo drive [E] Samsung SN-324

Slim-to-standard ATAPI/IDE adapter [F] For connecting a slim CD drive to standard PC motherboard connectors

PW-70 ATX power supply module [G] 70W, 12V DC-to-DC cableless converter for EPIA-M motherboards, available from iTuner (*store.ituner.com/ituner*)

AC-DC switching power adapter [H] 12V, 5A power adapter for PW-70 power supply module, available from iTuner (*store.ituner.com/ituner*)

ATX power extension cable Extension cable for use between EPIA-M motherboard and ATX power supply module

MPC II CD-ROM audio cable

Visit *makezine.com/02/atari* for source list.

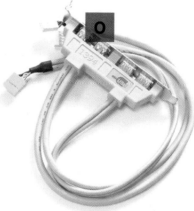

Stelladaptor Atari 2600 Controller-to-USB interface [J] (2) Designed by Pixels Past and available exclusively from AtariAge (*atariage.com*)

DB9 joystick extension cable (2) (optional)

USB four-port mini-hub [L] (optional) Needed only if using more than two internal USB accessories

Wireless keyboard and mouse (optional) Logitech Cordless Access Duo Optical

802.11b wireless USB adapter [N] (optional) D-Link DWL-122

Type A male-to-female USB cable extender (optional) Needed only with 802.11b wireless USB adapter

5.25- to 3.5-inch drive power adapter cable [Q]

5.25-inch drive power cable Y-splitter [R]

2.1mm ID, 5.5mm OD PCB-mount power jack [S] Digi-Key #CP-202A-ND

1"-wide double-sided foam tape 3M #4011, exterior mounting, super-strong

¾"-wide galvanized hanger strap Two to three feet; also known as pipe support or plumber's strapping tape

Spool of 22–26AWG wire Solid or stranded

6-32, ¾" threaded stand-off [W] (2) Aluminum or plastic with ¼" threaded post (for motherboard mounting)

6-32 nut (5) With optional lock washer (for CD-ROM drive and motherboard mounting)

6-32, ⅜" screw (5)

TOOLS:

Phillips screwdriver (regular and jeweler's size)

Flathead screwdriver (jeweler's size)

Dremel tool with cutting discs (also called cut-off wheels)

Drill with ⁹⁄₆₄" drill bit

X-ACTO/hobby knife

Soldering iron

Solder sucker or desoldering bulb

Needlenose pliers

Wire cutters/wire snips

Small flat file

Gorilla Glue

Hot glue gun

Liquid hand soap

Small metal scrub brush or toothbrush

Towel and washcloth

Protective gear (goggles, mask, gloves)

Compressed air (optional)

Photography by Joe Grand

MAKE IT.

MAKING THE ATARI 2600PC

BEFORE YOU START ⋯

GETTING TO KNOW YOUR SWITCHES

Before getting started, let's take a look at the four switches on the top of the Atari. They'll be used for the functions described below.

Number	1	2	3	4
Original Type	Toggle	Toggle	Momentary	Momentary
Original Function	Power on/off	TV type: Color/BW	Game select	Game reset
New Type	Momentary	—	Toggle	—
New Function	Power on/off	Unused	Unused	Wireless mouse/key-board
Notes	Replace with switch 3 (momentary) to work with motherboard	—	Replace with switch 1 (toggle)	—

Now, let's take a look at the back panel of the system. This explains their original functions, and how they'll be changed:

Number	1	3	5
Type	Slide	Slide	Slide
Original Function	Channel: 2/3	Right difficulty: A/B	Left difficulty: A/B
New Function	Unused	Unused	Unused
Notes			

Number	2	4	6
Type	DB-9	Jack	DB-9
Original Function	Right controller	Power	Left controller
New Function	Player 2 controller	Power	Player 1 controller
Notes	Interface with Stelladaptor	Replace with proper PC power supply jack	Interface with Stelladaptor

You'll want to refer back to these figures and tables as you go through the steps in the project. Now, with all your parts and tools organized and ready, we can begin the actual project. We'll first prepare all the individual components and then fit them all together.

START ⠿⠿

1. OPENING THE CASE

1a. Remove screws. To begin, remove the screws from the bottom of the 2600 using a standard Phillips screwdriver. There are four screws securing the case together.

Underside of the four-switch Atari 2600.

Note that the two bottom screws are longer, so you'll want to be sure to insert these into the correct holes when you are reassembling the unit.

1b. Open case. Once you have removed the screws, pull the two halves of the case apart, unplug the RF cable from the board, and remove the circuit board from the case. Since we'll be using some of the original connections on this board (the four switches on the top and the joystick connectors on the back) later on in the project, place the circuit board aside for now.

2. CLEANING THE CASE

Cleaning your case is the first step for a visually pleasing and successful case mod. Dirt and oils on the external case just don't look nice (and, if you plan to paint your case, will usually prevent paint from sticking). With the case in two plastic halves, you can either clean the pieces in the dishwasher by running them through a gentle cycle, or you can hand-wash them in a sink or bathtub. Since I don't have a dishwasher, I used a bathtub and regular liquid hand soap.

Rinse off dirt and dust.

Use a brush for small areas.

Once shiny, allow to dry.

3. MOCKING UP THE DESIGN

Before starting the modifications to the Atari case, we'll connect all the components together outside the case to make sure they function properly and without conflict. By mocking up the system like this, it will help you figure out if you need extra components and what parts (if any) you can discard. Also, by installing and configuring all the necessary software now, you'll find that when it's time to stuff all the components into the case, the computer will be ready to power up right away. Mocking up the design also acts as an early "burn-in" test, so if there are any faulty components, they'll hopefully fail now instead of once everything is fitted into the case.

Fitting all the components together is pretty straightforward and will vary depending on what parts you are using. If you have ever assembled a PC from parts before, the following steps should look familiar.

WARNING: HARDWARE HARM. Be sure to take proper antistatic precautions before working with electronic circuitry. All electronics should be handled only at a static-safe workstation with electrostatic discharge (ESD) mats and grounded wrist and ankle straps.

3a. Fit components together.

1. Insert the DRAM into the DIMM slot.

2. Attach the power supply module to the ATX power supply connector.

3. Connect the CD/DVD to the primary IDE connector using ATA133 cable supplied with Mini-ITX. This is after you connect the slim-to-standard ATAPI/IDE adapter.

4. Connect the hard drive to the secondary IDE connector using the 2.5-inch laptop IDE hard drive cable adapter.

5. Attach the power cables to the hard drive and CD/DVD.

6. Attach the USB/FireWire backplane to the yellow USB connector on the motherboard marked with "USB" on the top silkscreen.

7. Connect the USB hub and 802.11b wireless USB network interface card (NIC) to the USB ports on the backplane.

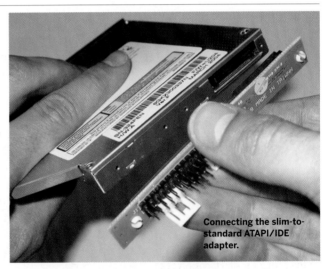
Connecting the slim-to-standard ATAPI/IDE adapter.

8. Connect the two Stelladaptors and the Logitech wireless mouse/keyboard receiver to the USB hub.

9. Attach a standard monitor, keyboard, and mouse.

10. Connect the DC power supply to the power connector.

3b. With all your components connected, your setup should look like this picture.

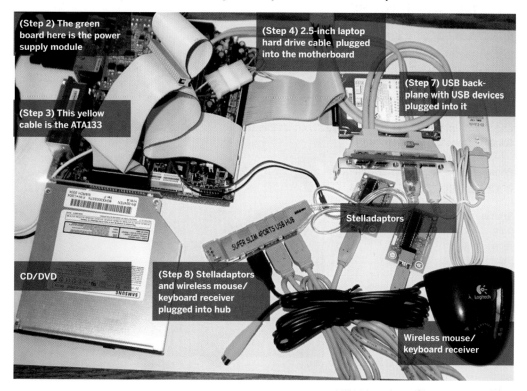

(Step 2) The green board here is the power supply module

(Step 4) 2.5-inch laptop hard drive cable plugged into the motherboard

(Step 7) USB back-plane with USB devices plugged into it

(Step 3) This yellow cable is the ATA133

Stelladaptors

CD/DVD

(Step 8) Stelladaptors and wireless mouse/keyboard receiver plugged into hub

Wireless mouse/keyboard receiver

3c. Turn on the computer. You'll need to use a jumper or screwdriver to momentarily short pins 6 and 8 of the F PANEL connector located near the PCI connector. The pinout to the F PANEL connector is shown in the user's manual provided with the motherboard. When we eventually fit the computer into the Atari case, those two pins will be soldered to the momentary Power On/Off switch on our control panel.

If the computer successfully powers on, the CPU fan will start spinning and you may hear your other devices coming to life. If the system does not start, immediately remove the power supply connection and recheck your connections to make sure they are all in the right places.

4. CONFIGURING THE BIOS

To enter the VIA BIOS configuration screen, hold down the Del key on your keyboard as soon as you power up the system. You will briefly see the EPIA logo and then be prompted with the screen for the Phoenix-AwardBIOS CMOS Setup Utility (see below). You might want to check the VIA website (www.via.com.tw) for the latest BIOS revision before you get started. From the BIOS menu, you can set the time, ensure that the motherboard is detecting your devices, and configure the motherboard for your particular specifications.

4a. Configure the motherboard.
For my configuration, I changed the following settings, but your changes could vary.

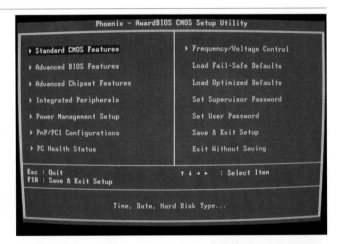

Standard CMOS Features
Date
Time
Drive A = NONE

Advanced CMOS Features
First boot device = CDROM
Second boot device = HDD-0
Third boot device = DISABLED
Boot other device = DISABLED
Display full-screen logo = DISABLED

Integrated Peripherals
Super IO device
Onboard FDC controller = DISABLED
Onboard LAN boot ROM = DISABLED

Power Management Setup
Power off by PWRBTN = Delay 4 Sec
Peripherals Activities
PS2KB wakeup from S3/S4/S5 = Ctrl+F1
PNP OS installed = YES

Note: Many of the Power Management Setup settings will be overridden by ACPI-aware operating systems such as Windows 98/98SE/ME/2000/XP.

With the BIOS configuration complete, insert the installation CD for your desired operating system, save the BIOS settings, and reboot the machine.

5. INSTALLING SOFTWARE

The process of configuring Windows and installing software applications is not covered in depth here. The applications you choose to install depend on how you intend to use the system. For my system, I split the 60GB drive into two partitions. The C: drive, aptly named Boring, is 10GB and will hold the Windows OS and all other applications. The E: drive, aptly named Fun, is approximately 50GB and will be used to store my movies, emulators, and game images.

5a. As a guideline, I installed the software in the following order:

1. Windows XP Professional

2. Windows XP Update: Service Pack 1a, critical updates and patches

3. VIA drivers (again, check the VIA website for the latest versions)

4. D-Link DWL-122 802.11 USB adapter drivers

5. Logitech cordless keyboard and mouse drivers

6. Nero 5 Burning ROM

7. PowerDVD XP

8. Emulators: MAME, z26, Atari800Win, MESS

With the cordless keyboard and mouse drivers installed, you can now remove the wired keyboard and mouse. When all the software is configured to your liking, the final step is to enable the TV output so you can attach the computer directly to a TV.

USING THE EPIA-M WITH A TV

When you first configure the VIA EPIA-M motherboard, it will only boot via the VGA connector and not through the TV output. This is a known issue between the EPIA-M series and Windows (which overrides the motherboard's display settings in the BIOS). Apparently, this is not an issue with Linux-based systems.

Once Windows has loaded, you can enable the TV output using the Control Panel Display dialog box. With the TV output mode enabled, you can boot the computer using only a TV and without the monitor. You only have to select these settings once, because they will be saved for future use.

To have a readable display on a TV, you might want to configure Windows to use the High-Contrast Black display setting at 800x600 resolution and set the system fonts to Large. The display settings aren't very conducive to performing actual work on the machine, but they are fine for selecting and controlling applications.

View of screen with Windows XP and software installed onto the PC.

6. PREPARING THE CONTROL PANEL

To prepare the original Atari circuit board for use in the Atari 2600PC, we first need to swap the toggle switch from the Power On/Off button (S201) with the momentary switch from the Game Select button (S203). This will give us the desired functionality described earlier. Having a spare Atari to use as parts can come in handy, in case you damage the switches while removing them from the board.

6a. Remove two switches from the Atari control panel. Before desoldering the switches, remove the four circular pads from the tops of each switch and place them aside. They are easily lost and you won't need them again until it is time to put the entire system back together. The two switches denoted with arrows should be removed.

There are six solder pads for each switch.

6b. Remove vertical traces from the switch pads. Before soldering the new switches into place, you need to cut two traces on each side of the circuit board. On both the front and back sides of the switch, marked S201 on the top silkscreen (the right-most switch if you are looking at the bottom of the circuit board, as in the photograph in step **6a**), use an X-ACTO knife to cut the two thick vertical traces that connect the two sets of pads. This will allow a momentary switch to be used in place of the original toggle switch.

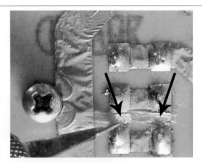

After the cuts, you should have six discrete pads, with none of the pads connected to any other.

6c. Bend the leads of the momentary switch to fit into the S201 footprint. The S203 momentary switch that is going into the S201 footprint is slightly too wide and won't fit in without modification. Simply use needle-nose pliers to bend the pins inward so they fit into the pads, and then solder them into place.

The momentary switch leads are too wide to fit into the S201 footprint.

6d. Insert the toggle switch you removed from the S201 into the inner pads of the S203 footprint and solder it into place.

6e. Replace the power connector at J201 with the correct size for our DC power supply. In the case of the iTuner PW-70, a 2.1mm ID/5.5mm OD PCB mount power jack (Digi-Key #CP-202A-ND) works just fine.

Here are the front and side views of the new PCB mount power jack.

6f. Remove the side lead from the power jack. Bend the side lead up and cut it completely off.

6g. Enlarge the circuit board holes for J201. The holes on the circuit board for the original J201 are too narrow to fit the new power jack, so we need to increase the width of the holes. Using a ⅛" drill bit in a Dremel tool or drill, drill out the bottom two holes (when the board is rotated 180 degrees and the connectors are facing you, as shown).

before

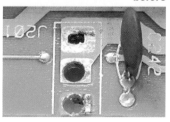

after

Here's the J201's circuit board before and after drilling the larger holes.

6h. Solder the power jack. The power jack should now fit into the circuit board. When it does, solder it into place.

And here's the circuit board with the new power jack soldered onto the board.

6i. Add hot glue to the connectors for reinforcement. Due to the old age and typically high wear of the components, you should use some hot glue around the edges of all the connectors on the back to reinforce them and add some strain relief.

6j. Remove the radio frequency (RF) shielding. To do this, use a pair of needlenose pliers to twist the small metal tabs along the edges of the RF shield so that the tabs line up with the slots in the shield. You should then be able to pull the two halves of the shield apart from both sides of the circuit board.

Once the RF shield is removed, the board should resemble the one shown here. You can discard the shield, since we aren't using it for this project.

6k. Cut the Atari 2600 circuit board. Use a Dremel tool to remove the unnecessary circuitry (which takes up valuable space within the Atari case). Before cutting, remove the integrated circuit (IC) located in the socket near the C201 marking, directly underneath the cartridge connector. This will make it easier to cut the circuit board. We want to keep the connectors, switches, and cartridge connector in place while removing everything else. To mark the cut, simply flip the board over to the solder side (where there are no components) and draw a straight line across the board with a permanent marker. As shown here, cut horizontally across the circuit board, about 2½" down from the top of the board (where the connectors are located).

Be sure to wear goggles during this step, because stray component pieces and fiberglass from the circuit board can lead to injury.

6l. Inspect your work. You should now have a long, narrow control panel with all the necessary switches and connectors, as shown here.

The control panel. You're almost done.

6m. Remove the rest of the extraneous circuit board material from the control panel. This creates additional vertical space within the Atari housing, which we'll need later.

6n. Use wire snips to remove all the discrete components (capacitors, resistors, and inductors) from the board. Anything that isn't a switch or a connector should be removed; if one of these old, unused components fails, the operation of the PC could possibly be affected.

6o. Clean the plastic cartridge connector. It is usually encrusted with decades of dirt. Use the hand towel and liquid hand soap and be careful not to get soap or water into the switches or connectors on the back. The cartridge connector isn't used for our project, but it is visible from the outside when the case is closed, so we want it to look nice.

The control panel preparations are finally complete.

7. PREPARING THE USB/FIREWIRE BACKPLANE

The VIA EPIA M10000 motherboard comes with a USB/FireWire backplane, which contains the additional connectors for two FireWire (IEEE1394) and two USB ports. Space is hard to come by inside the Atari housing, so to reduce the amount of area that the connectors need, we will do a slight modification to remove the FireWire ports that we aren't using. If you have FireWire devices you want to connect to the system, you might not want to perform this step.

7a. Remove the three screws that hold on the metal PCI expansion card rail.

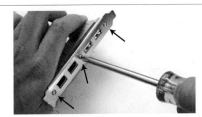

Get rid of the rail; you won't need it.

7b. Cut the backplane in half, removing the unneeded FireWire ports. Also, cut off the extraneous plastic from the other side of the USB ports.

Be careful not to cut too closely to any of the connectors; you don't want to damage the connectors or wires.

7c. Inspect your work. When you're done, the backplane should resemble the one shown here.

8. PREPARING THE CORDLESS KEYBOARD/MOUSE RECEIVER

Next, let's remove all the unneeded plastic housings surrounding the receiver unit supplied with the Logitech Cordless Access Duo optical keyboard and mouse.

8a. Open the unit by unscrewing the single screw on the back of the device and prying off the top half of the plastic housing.

One screw secures the top half of the cordless receiver to the base.

8b. Remove unneeded pieces, specifically the housing and the extra plastic piece sitting on top of the five LEDs at the front of the unit. Then remove the whole circuit board from the bottom housing.

The plastic housing and extra plastic piece can be discarded.

8c. Cut the connector cable stress relief. The receiver unit comes with both USB and PS/2 connectors. Because we'll only be using the USB connector, the PS/2 cable and connector can be removed, since it only takes up space.

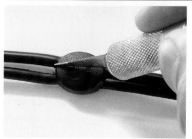

Be careful not to let the knife slip and cut into either of the wires.

First, use an X-ACTO knife to cut the plastic, oval-shaped Logitech stress relief in half. Slicing through the middle of the stress relief will allow you to separate the two cables. The stress relief is located where the two separate USB and PS/2 cables join.

8d. Split the cable all the way down to the circuit board by lightly pulling on each side of the cable.

8e. Cut off the cable connected to the PS/2 connector. The USB connector and wire should be left in place, as shown at right.

8f. Add an extension from the push-button switch on the receiver to a momentary switch on the control panel. Simply solder an 18- to 20-inch length of 22-26AWG wire to each of the two pads shown here. The polarity of the wires does not matter. Wrap the wires through the hole on the right side of the circuit board, to act as a strain relief.

The wires will be connected to the Atari control panel later in the project.

This way, the connect functionality (used to enable the wireless connection between the keyboard/mouse and the PC) can be activated without having to leave the wireless receiver accessible outside the case.

The modification of the cordless keyboard/mouse receiver is now complete.

IN THE BEGINNING

In 1977, when Atari introduced the Video Computer System (VCS) — later renamed the 2600 — nobody, not even Atari, knew it would ultimately become a wild success and be the catalyst that would spawn the multibillion-dollar gaming industry we know today. It was one of the first generation of videogame systems that was not hardwired to play a certain set of games; today it is recognized around the world as the classic gaming system. Besides an unofficial Atari History Museum (atarimuseum.com), there are a multitude of fan clubs around the world and approximately 10,000 websites, including AtariAge (atariage.com).

Last year, Atari itself began tapping into the nostalgia with its Atari Flashback Classic Game Console, which revives 2600 (and 7800) faves such as Breakout, Battlezone, and Millipede.

9. PREPARING THE STELLADAPTOR 2600 CONTROLLER-TO-USB INTERFACES

The Stelladaptor 2600 Controller-to-USB Interface, designed by Pixels Past (pixelspast.com), allows the use of standard Atari 2600-compatible controllers, including joysticks, paddles, and driving controllers, with modern computers running Windows, Macintosh, or Linux operating systems. Adding the Stelladaptor support into our Atari 2600 case mod will allow us to plug the original Atari controllers into the back of the 2600, just like in the old days, and use them with emulators running on the PC. It adds another point of authenticity to the case mod. **Two Stelladaptor units are required:** one for Player 1 and one for Player 2. The following instructions should be repeated for each unit.

9a. Pry open the Stelladaptor. To prepare the Stelladaptor, you first need to remove the external plastic housing. You can do this using a small flathead jeweler's screwdriver to simply separate the two halves at the denoted latch points.

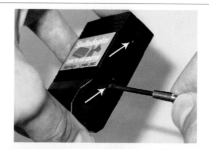

9b. Remove the Stelladaptor circuitry from its shell. When the device is opened, you can discard the plastic housing. You'll be left with a single circuit board, as shown.

9c. Desolder the DB9 connector from the Stelladaptor. To conserve space inside the Atari case, we will replace the DB9 connectors with nine discrete wires. Later on in the project, those wires will be soldered directly to the pads of the original Atari's DB9 joystick connectors on the control panel. First, remove the DB9 connector from the Stelladaptor circuit board.

The DB9 is denoted as P1 on the silkscreen, but it is hard to miss (it's on the right side of the photograph in 9b, underneath the thumb).

9d. Modify the Stelladaptor with wire connections. Next, using nine 8-inch lengths of 22-26AWG wire, solder the wires into the DB9 pads on the Stelladaptor circuit board. If you have one available, use a DB9 joystick extension cable with the ends cut off, which has nine wires in a sheath.

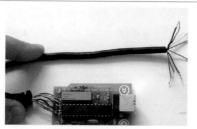

The Stelladaptor modifications are complete. At this point, you should have two identical units that each resemble the one shown.

10. PREPARING THE POWER SUPPLY CONNECTOR

Two simple modifications to the iTuner PW70 ATX power supply module are required to prepare it for the case mod.

10a. Gather the iTuner PW70 ATX power supply module and DC converter.

10b. Remove the 12VDC power supply input connector from the PW70. The black-and-white pair of wires on the PW70 serves as the 12VDC power supply input to the module. If a connector is provided with your module, cut it off as close to the connector as possible. Later on in the project, the white (+12VDC input) and black (GND) wires will be soldered directly to the power supply jack that is mounted to the control panel.

10c. Remove the red-and-black two-wire connector from the PW70. The PW70 module also comes with a connector (the 2-pin connector with red and black leads) that provides +5VDC for optional user applications. Since this connector isn't needed in the project, it can be removed.

The red and black wires to cut are on the lower-right corner of the module's circuit board, as shown. Cut the leads off as close to the circuit board as possible (or desolder the red and black connections from the board) and put it aside for now. The 2-pin connector fits perfectly on the front panel (F PANEL) header on the PC motherboard, so the connector and wires will be reused for our Power On/Off switch later on.

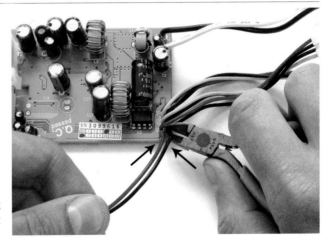

10d. Inspect your work. The modified PW70 power supply module should resemble the one shown here.

11. PREPARING THE MINI-ITX MOTHERBOARD

Due to the lack of vertical clearance in the Atari housing, the ATX power connector on the motherboard needs to be modified so it will fit properly within the housing.

A modified ATX power extension cable will be used to extend the power from the iTuner PW70 power supply module onto the motherboard. This modification prevents us from taking advantage of the "cableless" solution of the PW70 (which is designed to plug directly into the ATX power connector on the motherboard), but it's all in the name of hacking!

WARNING: HARDWARE HARM. Be careful when removing the ATX power connector from the EPIA-M motherboard. The motherboard contains dozens of tiny, densely packed components. Any stress on the board could cause parts to come loose or become damaged. Also, take care not to scratch or damage any PCB traces.

11a. Remove the ATX power connector. First, completely remove the plastic ATX power connector from the motherboard (denoted as ATXPWR on the silkscreen). By removing the connector, you'll gain approximately half an inch of vertical clearance.

These three photos show the EPIA-M motherboard before the ATX power connector was removed, while the connector is being desoldered, and after the successful removal.

11b. Remove the male connector from the ATX extension cable. This is the side that looks the same as the connector mounted on the PW70 power supply module. Each of the 20 wires will be soldered to the bottom of the Mini-ITX motherboard, giving the necessary vertical clearance on the top of the motherboard.

11c. Strip insulation from the wires. Once the connector is removed, strip about ¼" of insulation from each wire. Twist the stranded wires at the end of each lead on the ATX extension cable and "tin" them with a small amount of solder.

The ATX extension cable is ready to be soldered to the motherboard.

11d. Solder wires to the motherboard. Now the modified extension cable is ready to be inserted and soldered into the motherboard. Luckily, each connection is designated with its function on the bottom silkscreen of both the motherboard and the power supply module, so it is easy to see where they connect (for example, +5V to +5V, GND to GND, -12V to -12V, and so on). Although the wire colors of the ATX extension cable may vary, mine were laid out in the following fashion:

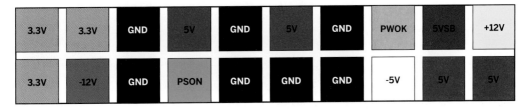

3.3V	3.3V	GND	5V	GND	5V	GND	PWOK	5VSB	+12V
3.3V	-12V	GND	PSON	GND	GND	GND	-5V	5V	5V

11e. Inspect your work. When the extension cable is soldered into the motherboard, the modified EPIA-M motherboard should resemble the one shown here.

12. PREPARING THE HOUSING

This section is the messiest and most time consuming, but when you're done, you'll have an Atari 2600 case waiting with open arms and ready to be stuffed full of PC components.

12a. Remove the plastic tabs. This photograph shows the Atari 2600 bottom housing with arrows pointing to the seven areas where plastic needs to be removed. Removing the unnecessary plastic will give us more space inside the case so we can fit all the parts inside.

With the plastic pieces successfully removed, your case should resemble the one shown below.

Using the Dremel tool and cutting wheel, remove the two large recessed screw holes/struts located near the back of the case. When you remove these pieces, there will be two oval holes going out through the bottom of the case. Next, remove the two thin posts located in front of those struts and the lone post on the right edge of the case. Also, remove the wire stress relief post on the upper-right side of the case. Finally, remove the top section of the wire stress relief column on the lower-right side of the case. Remove only the top two plastic ovals. The bottom cylinder should be left in place because it will act as the hard drive support later on.

12b. Prepare the case to hold the motherboard and the CD-ROM drive. Since the CD-ROM drive will be sitting below the motherboard, it's the first thing that needs to be mounted. The CD-ROM drive will be situated facing the front of the case, so it will open straight toward you. Align the drive in the center of the case and use a permanent marker to outline the rectangular area that will need to be removed from the front of the case.

Because the drive is slim, it fits perfectly under the lip of the bottom housing, doesn't interfere with the wood-grain bezel, and is fairly unobtrusive, so it won't be obvious that the Atari 2600 has been modified.

12c. Carefully Dremel out the marked area. It is easiest to do this from the inside of the case, slightly within your marked rectangle. Then use a small file to flatten out the sides right up to the edges of the markings.

You should now have a nice rectangle under the front lip of the housing through which the CD-ROM tray can fit.

12d. Mark the motherboard location on the back of the Atari 2600 bottom housing. Place the motherboard inside the bottom housing and use a permanent marker to outline the rectangular area of the connector panel that will need to be removed from the back of the case. Be sure that the CD-ROM drive is sitting in place first, because the motherboard will be sitting on top of it and will be lifted slightly off the bottom of the case.

The motherboard will be situated inside the housing with its connectors facing the back of the case. This way, any physical connections will be out of sight. In order for the motherboard's connector panel to be accessible, the back of the Atari housing will need to be modified. We'll prepare the bottom of the Atari housing first and work on mating the top housing later.

12e. Once again, carefully Dremel out the marked area, as explained in step 12c.

Finally, cut a slot in the left support post (see arrow), which will enable the motherboard to slide all the way, flush with the back of the case, making the connectors easier to access once the case is closed.

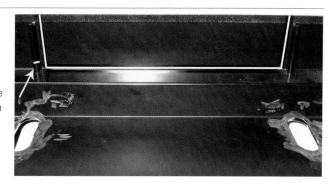

12f. Drill locations for motherboard mounting holes. To mount the mother-board to the bottom of the Atari case, you need to drill three holes (see arrows). The diameter of the holes will vary depending on the diameter of your standoffs and screws. I used a ⁹⁄₆₄" drill bit for the 6-32 size hardware.

Don't screw anything together quite yet. Later in the project, the two screw holes on the front of the motherboard will be screwed into place with standoffs, and the screw hole in the back corner will be fastened with a nut and bolt.

12g. Inspect your work. The completed bottom Atari 2600 housing should resemble the one shown here. Now we can move on to the top half of the Atari housing.

12h. Enlarge the case to fit the new power jack. First, the original hole in the back of the case intended for the power jack needs to be enlarged. The new power jack that was soldered on during the control panel preparation is slightly larger than the original Atari one. Simply use a small, flat file to enlarge the square hole in the back of the case (left image) until the new power jack fits snugly through it (right image).

Remove the control panel after the jack has been successfully enlarged; we'll screw it into place later in the project.

12i. Use the Dremel to remove the four "ribs" on the underside of the top housing. They take up much needed vertical space, and the motherboard will not have enough room to fit inside unless they are removed.

12j. Place the CD-ROM drive and motherboard back into the bottom housing. Don't mount them yet — this step is just for measurement purposes. Set the top half of the housing on top, as though you were putting the case back together. It won't fit fully yet, because the connectors on the back are too high.

12k. Dremel out the marked area. Use a permanent marker to outline the rectangular area that needs to be cut from the top housing so that the whole connector panel will fit through the back. The rectangle will be approximately 9/16" high and 5¾" long, centered with the rectangle cut of the bottom housing. Next, carefully Dremel out the marked area. It is easiest to do this from the inside of the case, slightly within your marked rectangle. Then use a small file to flatten out the sides right up to the edges of the markings.

12l. Cut a large notch horizontally across the underside of the Atari 2600 top housing so that the DRAM can fit inside without hitting the top of the case. Without this modification, the DRAM is too high and will prevent the case from closing properly. The location of the notch may vary slightly, depending on how you mount your motherboard. Using a Dremel tool, enlarge the slits on the underside of the case, approximately where the DRAM hits the top (you can try to stick your finger through the hole in the back of the case and feel around to where the DRAM is located). Here, the locations are denoted by arrows.

Take care not to remove too much plastic from the slits, since you might end up with cuts appearing on the top side of the housing.

13. PUTTING IT ALL TOGETHER

Now that all the preparations have been completed, it's time to move on to cramming everything into the Atari case. Remember, this is a project, so there is more than one "right" way to do things. If after following these directions something doesn't fit as you like, don't be afraid to experiment with other methods to place and mount the components. The case mod is ultimately a reflection of you and your personality.

WARNING: HARDWARE HARM. Be sure to take proper antistatic precautions before working with the electronic circuitry. All electronics should be handled only at a static-safe workstation with ESD mats and grounded wrist and ankle straps.

THE CD-ROM DRIVE

13a. Make and secure the drive-mounting rail. First, we need to mount the CD-ROM drive to the bottom of the Atari housing. Cut an 8" length of the hanger strap and fold it around the top of the drive so it fits like a brace. Try to make it as snug fitting as possible without creating undue stress on the top or sides of the drive. Using Gorilla Glue, glue the brace to the top of the drive. Clamp or weigh down the strap with a few heavy books and wait three or four hours for the glue to cure. Be careful that the books aren't so heavy that they warp the top of the drive.

The hanger strap will act as our drive rail.

Tip: Slightly moisten the top of the drive with some water before applying the glue.

13b. Drill the mounting holes. When the glue is dry, align the CD-ROM drive with the slot hole you prepared earlier. Use a permanent marker to mark one hole on each side of the drive rail onto the bottom of the Atari case. Using the proper drill bit — size based on the nut diameter you are using (I used a ⁹⁄₆₄" bit for the 6-32 screw) — simply drill out the two holes.

13c. Attach the DVD drive. Next, insert the two screws from the underside of the Atari case and attach the nut on top of the drive rail. With the two screws in place, the CD-ROM should be securely mounted and should not wiggle or move in any direction.

Take care not to over-tighten the screws, placing stress across the top of the CD-ROM drive, which could cause disc vibration or rattling when the entire system is put together.

13d. Connect the cable to the back of the drive. Because the 3.5-inch drive PC power connector on the PW70 power supply module (used to connect to the slim CD-ROM drive) is too short and won't reach to the drive, we need to create an extension cable using the 5.25- to 3.5-inch drive power adapter cable and a 5.25-inch drive power cable Y-splitter. Connect the power, audio, and IDE cable to the back of the drive.

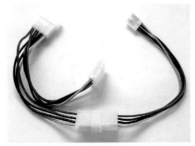

With the custom power cable extension, there is ample length to connect it between the power supply module and the slim CD-ROM drive.

THE MOTHERBOARD

13e. Attach motherboard. Align the motherboard into the bottom of the Atari housing. The connectors should be facing out the back, as flush to the edge as possible. To secure the motherboard, first insert a screw from the bottom into the motherboard-mounting hole next to the connectors on the back panel. Insert a nut from the top of the motherboard and tighten it into place. Next, place the two ¾" standoffs underneath the two front mounting holes, insert the nuts from the top of the motherboard, and tighten them. From the underside of the case, insert a screw into each of the two holes and loosely screw them in.

13f. Connect the ATA133 and audio cables from the CD-ROM to the motherboard. Both cables should come out from underneath the left side of the motherboard. The audio cable should plug into the mating audio connector (labeled "CD IN" on the silkscreen). Flip the ATA133 cable over and connect it to the IDE connector marked "PRIMARY" on the silkscreen.

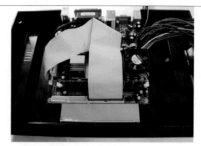

THE HARD DRIVE

We'll mount the hard drive to the case with pieces of foam tape. The tape is extremely strong and will hold with typical use of the PC. It also serves double duty as a shock absorber. Velcro could also be used for easier removal of the hard drive, if you're planning to upgrade at a later date.

13g. Attach foam tape to the underside of the drive. First, attach the IDE cable to the back of the drive. Then, attach a 3¾" length of foam tape to the bottom left side of the hard drive.

Remove the protective coating from the bottom side of the foam tape and mount the drive to the front left area of the bottom Atari housing. The foam tape will stick to the lip of the plastic. The IDE connector of the drive should be facing toward the back of the case.

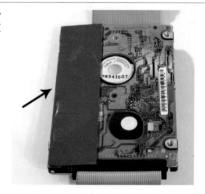

13h. Connect wires to F PANEL pins. Before connecting the IDE cable to the motherboard, retrieve the two-wire red and black cable you cut off the iTuner power supply module. Plug it into pins 6 and 8 of the header marked F PANEL on the silkscreen. The header is immediately next to the hard drive.

It doesn't matter which orientation the connector goes on, since both leads will be connected to the momentary power switch on the control panel later in the project.

13i. Connect the IDE cable to the drive. Finally, flip the IDE cable over the hard drive and connect it to the IDE connector marked "SECONDARY" on the silkscreen (the connector closest to the drive).

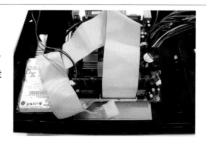

THE PW70 POWER SUPPLY MODULE

Fitting the PW70 power supply module into the case is one of the trickiest aspects of this project. The ATX connector is quite high compared to the amount of free vertical space we have inside the Atari case, so finding the best location to mount the unit might take a bit of tweaking.

13j. Connect the ATX extension cable (which is now soldered to the motherboard) into the ATX connector of the power supply module. Next, place the power supply module upside down at the front right corner of the Atari housing. Feed the cables underneath the module to reach the power connectors of the CD-ROM and hard drive. The black and white wires should also be brought toward the back of the system, since they will be soldered onto the power connector on the control panel later in the project. The module should stay in its place without any mounting materials, but you might want to tack it down with a little bit of hot glue just so it doesn't move around as you continue placing components into the housing.

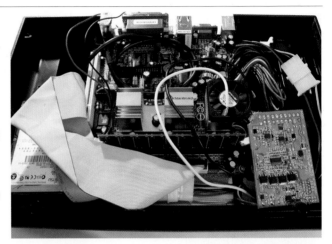

The power supply module mounted into the Atari 2600 (front right corner).

13k. Plug the PC power connectors into the hard drive and CD-ROM

THE USB COMPONENTS

The next step is to cram all the USB components into the case. This includes the mini four-port USB hub, cordless keyboard/mouse receiver, 802.11b NIC, and two Stelladaptors. These parts will essentially fit wherever they can inside the case. Since they are all connected via standard USB cables, there will be sufficient length to place the devices in every nook and cranny within the housing.

13l. Plug in the modified USB header into the yellow connector on the motherboard marked USB on the top silkscreen. Connect one side of the Type A male-to-female USB cable extender to the D-Link USB NIC, and connect the other side to one of the connectors of the modified USB header.

13m. Attach a 2" piece of foam tape to the underside of the D-Link USB NIC. This device fits perfectly in the empty area directly underneath the hard drive. Carefully slide it underneath and press it down to secure it to the bottom housing.

13n. Attach a 4" piece of foam tape to the underside of the mini four-port USB hub. Mount the unit lengthwise on the back left side of the Atari case, behind the hard drive. One end of the mini-hub actually sits on top of the hard drive and angles downward toward the back of the case. Be careful not to cover the hole on the hard drive marked with a "DO NOT COVER" warning. This is an air vent for the drive; if covered, it can cause the drive to overheat and/or fail. Connect the mini-hub connector to the other remaining connection on the modified USB header.

13o. Mount the cordless keyboard/mouse receiver circuit board to the top of the hard drive. Place two short lengths of foam tape across the solder side of the circuit board (the side with no components). Then, press it down on top of the hard drive, again taking care not to cover the hole on the hard drive marked with a "DO NOT COVER" warning.

13p. Mount the two Stelladaptors into the back right corner of the housing, above the tangle of wires coming from the ATX power supply connector. Both Stelladaptors can fit nicely standing on their sides. Run the USB cable from each Stelladaptor across the motherboard in front of the processor and heat sink, and connect it into the mini-hub. Position the Stelladaptors as shown, with the USB connector toward the front of the case and the nine wires toward the back. Use hot glue to fix the modules into place.

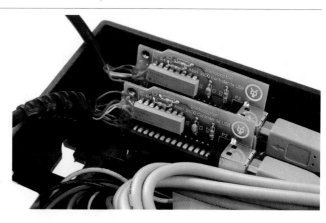

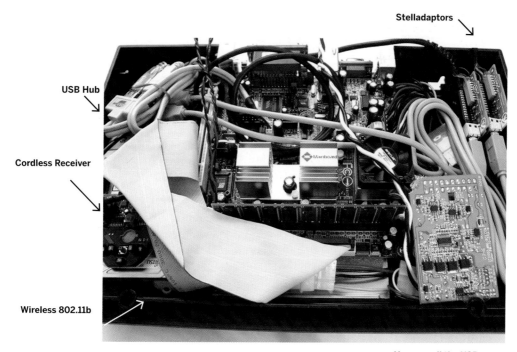

Stelladaptors

USB Hub

Cordless Receiver

Wireless 802.11b

Here are all the USB components mounted into the Atari 2600.

THE CONTROL PANEL

Remember that control panel we spent so long preparing at the beginning of the project? Well, it's time to mount it into the case. Before doing so, don't forget to replace the four circular pads onto the tops of each switch. With the control panel in place, use two of the screws you set aside when you opened the case and screw them into the two holes in the control panel.

The control panel mounted to the Atari 2600 top housing.

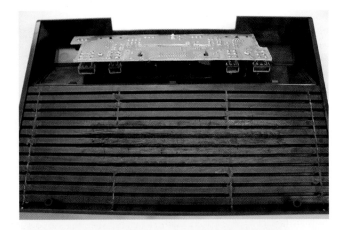

The Atari 2600 housings aligned and ready for connections.

14. SOLDERING WIRES ONTO THE CONTROL PANEL

Now we need to solder all the control panel-related wires onto the control panel. The easiest way to attach the wires is to lay the top of the Atari housing (now containing the control panel) upside down, facing back to back with the bottom of the Atari housing, as shown in the previous photograph. This way, you have easy access to both the top and bottom housings and the necessary wires and solder pads.

14a. Connect wires to the Power On/Off switch. First, solder the red and black leads from the F PANEL header to the two upper left pads of the S201 momentary power switch (on the far left of the control panel, if you're looking at the solder side of the circuit board, as shown here).

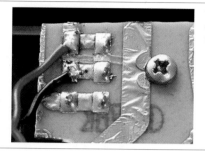

The polarity of the connections does not matter for this switch.

14b. Connect wires to the cordless keyboard/mouse connect switch. Now, solder the two wires from the cordless keyboard/mouse extension cable to the two upper left pads of the S202 momentary switch (on the far right of the control panel, if you're looking at the solder side of the circuit board).

14c. Connect wires to power jack. Next, solder the black and white wires from the power supply module onto the power jack of the control panel. The black (GND) wire connects to the front pad (closest to you, as shown here) and the white (+12VDC) connects to the other pad. The polarity of the connections is crucial in this step. Ensure that the black and white wires are connected to the proper pads before applying power to the system.

Make sure you solder the black and white wires to the correct pads in this step.

14d. Attach the nine wires from each Stelladaptor to the DB9 connectors on the control panel. Solder pin 1 to pin 1, pin 2 to pin 2, and so on for each Stelladaptor-to-DB9 connection. Make sure that you note the proper pinout of the DB9 connectors before you solder your wires. It is easy to confuse the order and direction of the pins. If your Stelladaptors don't work properly when you've finished your project, incorrect ordering of the wires is the most likely problem.

14e. Hot glue the connections. With all the wires soldered to the control panel, cover the connections with hot glue to protect and reinforce them. The hot glue will also serve as a strain relief to prevent the wires from breaking when you are closing the Atari case.

At this point, we've made all the connections for the project and we can button up the case!

Your control panel should now have three pairs of wires and the DB9 connections soldered to it. It should resemble the system shown here.

15. CLOSING UP THE CASE

15a. Make sure all the components and cables are properly connected. Now would be a good time to test the PC's functionality again, to make sure everything works as it did before it was force-fit into the case.

15b. Place the top housing onto the bottom housing, taking extreme care not to crush or pinch any wires or components, or accidentally bend the motherboard. If the case does not close easily, take a peek inside to see what is preventing it from doing so. Chances are, it's just something simple like a wire or cable getting in the way. Move things around until the case closes nicely. If there is another problem, remove the top housing and remedy the situation. Take care not to crush the CD-ROM drive, the DRAM, or the motherboard when you are cramming the case halves together.

15c. Make foam tape "hinges." Once the case halves fit together, you will notice that the back half is still slightly open since the original screw mounts were removed from the bottom of the case in order to fit the motherboard. Use two short lengths of foam tape on the inside back halves of the case to hold the back shut. The foam tape will act as a hinge. If you are feeling ambitious, you can use two short lengths of the hanger strap to create hinges, drilling them into the inside back of the case and mounting them with screws and nuts. Either method works just fine, though the hanger strap will be sturdier than the foam tape and won't deform with heat.

CONGRATULATIONS! The case modification is complete.

FINISH X

NOW GO USE IT »

Reprinted with permission from *Game Console Hacking*, copyright 2004, Syngress Publishing, ISBN: 1931836310, pp. 19-83.

USE IT.

GETTING THE MOST OUT OF YOUR RETRO PC

NOTES ABOUT THE SYSTEM

The Atari 2600PC boots rapidly and has no problem running the various emulators and CyberLink's included PowerDVD player. If connected to a computer monitor, the Atari 2600PC could easily be used for traditional PC tasks, such as surfing the web, sending and receiving email, and word processing, all without noticeable lag.

The system is connected to my home wireless network, which makes it a snap to load updated emulators and new game ROMs onto it. When I play DVDs, which uses a fair amount of computational power, the system gets pretty hot. However, I have yet to experience any problems with overheating. Cooling features could always be retrofitted to the project, if necessary.

My main concern is that the wireless keyboard/mouse, now that it has been modified, has a range of only about one foot compared to the original six feet it had before modification. This could be due to electrical noise or the fact that the receiver is blocked by the thick plastic Atari housing. So, I've resorted to using a wired USB keyboard and mouse at certain times, unless I'm directly in front of the system.

As a final touch, you could pick up a new, old-stock original Atari dust cover (model #CB101188-GL) from Best Electronics (best-electronics-ca.com). It is brown vinyl with a gold Atari logo. This way, the unit won't get too dusty when it isn't in use, and the dust cover looks cool, too.

Enjoy your new retro PC!

FINDING AN ATARI 2600

The Atari system itself doesn't need to work, since we won't be using the actual circuitry — we're just hacking some of the switches and connectors.

During my frequent visits to flea markets (another obsession of mine), I picked up four Atari 2600 systems — one working six-switch model for $20 and three four-switch models for $5 and $1.

The key is that the case be in good physical condition and look nice. Also, I made sure that the switches on top (two toggle and two momentary for the four-switch, and four toggle and two momentary for the six-switch) moved properly and that the connectors in back were not cracked or damaged in any way. If you live in an area without decent flea markets or computer surplus stores, buying a used Atari 2600 online is the next best option. eBay (ebay.com) and Yahoo! Auctions (auctions.yahoo.com) are both good starting points, as are vintage game specialists such as AtariAce (atariace.com) and 8-Bit Classics (8bitclassics.com). You shouldn't have much trouble finding a system for $5 to $50.

STUFFING PCS INTO VIDEOGAME SYSTEM CONSOLES

There has always been something cool about creating a usable computer system from an old videogame console. The following list has a few of the interesting ones that other people have worked on:

NESPC mini-itx.com/projects/nespc
Atari 800 ITX mini-itx.com/projects/atari800
AnimalSNES mini-itx.com/projects/animalsnes
PlayStation PC mini-itx.com/projects/playstationpc
PlayStation2 PC mini-itx.com/projects/playstation2pc
Dreamcast PC mini-itx.com/projects/dreamcastpc
Saturn PC mini-itx.com/projects/saturnpc

TOOLS FOR ATARI 2600 HOMEBREW GAMES

By Simon Carless

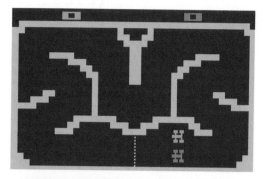

Even though the Atari 2600 is one of the oldest game consoles around, it has a vibrant homebrew scene. These coders produce a remarkable amount of new material, with everything from RPGs to bizarre puzzle games to altered updatings of classics. Best of all, the Atari 2600 scene seems to exist in an atmosphere of harmony and mutual understanding, with no beefs, group wars, or other shenanigans.

How can you create new game levels for the 2600? Good question.

Atari Age runs a series of excellent contests in which you can create new levels for games under development. Often, the finished and produced homebrew cartridge will include the winning levels. More importantly, entrants often make their tools available after the contest closes.

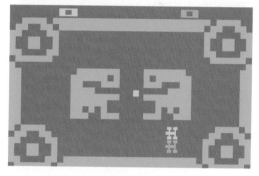

In particular, the Indy 500 XE Track Designer, atariage.com/features/contests/Indy500XE, is a lot of fun if you're a wannabe race driver. The "easy-to-use Windows-based track editor allows the easy creation of new tracks, loading and saving of tracks … and the ability to generate a binary so you can immediately test your creations."

The Combat Redux Playfield Design tool, atariage.com/features/ contests/CombatRedux, works similarly. It's a whole lot of fun to block out a level and then test it straightaway in an emulator.

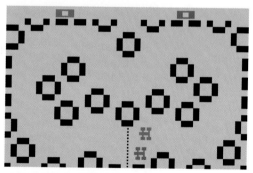

These two appear to be the only fully featured level design tools currently available. Other tools require complex, time-consuming binary hacking, such as atariage.com/software_hacks.html. However, it looks like the development community may produce further advanced tools, with an Adventure dungeon editor under serious development as we write — and more tools are planned.

The exhaustive Atari Age even has the last word with regard to coding resources, with an excellent coding page (atariage.com/2600/programming) that links to Kirk Israel's superlative 2600 101 basic tutorial (atariage.com/2600/programming/2600_101).

As for already produced homebrew titles, go to Atari Age's 2600 search page, pick Homebrew from the Rarity drop-down menu, and hit the Search button, atariage.com/software_search.html.

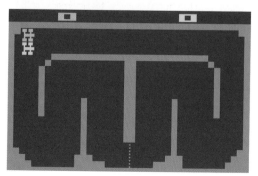

PODCASTING 101

By Phillip Torrone

Produce and syndicate audio interviews you record online, on the phone, and on the road. >>

Chris Pirillo (left) and Jake Ludington of the Chris Pirillo show. www.thechrispirilloshow.com

MAKE YOUR
OWN PODCAST

Podcasting gives me the feeling that I have the keys to NPR; that I can interview anyone I want and then deliver it over the internet to anyone who wants to listen in.

Podcasting involves producing your own audio files (usually in MP3, Ogg, or WMA formats) and then publishing them online somewhere, indexed for subscription and reception by an RSS (Really Simple Syndication) reader. They're then downloaded to subscribers' iPods, cellphones, iTunes directories, or other locations to listen to whenever they want. As you'll see, anyone can do this, using all free tools.

The podcasting genre particularly shines for interviews. I've interviewed *makers* from around the world via Skype or iChat (plus in person) and made them available as podcasts. Check out MAKE: Audio on makezine.com for lots of examples.

Phillip Torrone is associate editor of MAKE and producer of MAKE: Audio, all the DIY audio you can shake an iPod at. You can check out his blog as well as his audio work on *makezine.com*.

'CASTING CALLS

Want to become a leading cultural voice in your spare time, and without spending any money? Here's how.

Interviews and other talk audio will record well in mono, with a relatively low sampling rate. So you can do it in person or remotely, using non-professional equipment, and it'll sound just fine. Global reach, zero cost. Talk it up!

Once you've recorded your interview, you can trim it, add introductory material and music, and do whatever else you want using an audio mixing application such as Audacity. When you've finished editing your segment, export it to a standard download format such as MP3 or Ogg Vorbis.

After tagging the file with basic information about your show (and optional extras like artwork), upload it to your public server directory. People who catch the podcasting bug will soon build up an impressive collection.

Your RSS file lists and timestamps the set of podcasts that you have available. This allows your audience's podcatcher software to determine which ones are new and prime for downloading. By keeping it fresh, frequent podcasters automatically get more downloads.

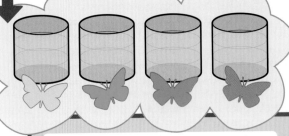

HOW TO RECEIVE: To subscribe to a podcast, paste its one-line RSS address into your podcatcher application. There's no charge. The app makes periodic rounds and collects new broadcasts for you. If it's good, that's great, and if not, just delete it and move to the next one instantly.

Illustration by Tim Lillis

SET UP.

Visit *makezine.com/02/podcast* for source list.

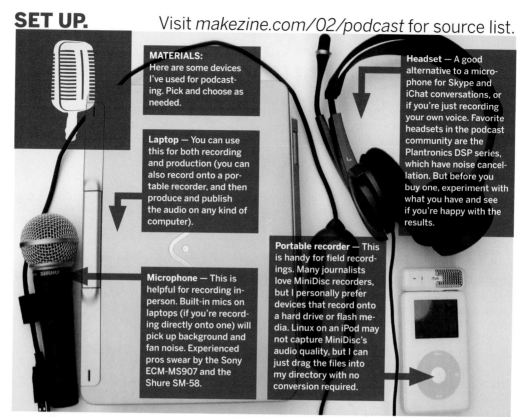

MATERIALS:
Here are some devices I've used for podcasting. Pick and choose as needed.

Laptop — You can use this for both recording and production (you can also record onto a portable recorder, and then produce and publish the audio on any kind of computer).

Microphone — This is helpful for recording in-person. Built-in mics on laptops (if you're recording directly onto one) will pick up background and fan noise. Experienced pros swear by the Sony ECM-MS907 and the Shure SM-58.

Portable recorder — This is handy for field recordings. Many journalists love MiniDisc recorders, but I personally prefer devices that record onto a hard drive or flash media. Linux on an iPod may not capture MiniDisc's audio quality, but I can just drag the files into my directory with no conversion required.

Headset — A good alternative to a microphone for Skype and iChat conversations, or if you're just recording your own voice. Favorite headsets in the podcast community are the Plantronics DSP series, which have noise cancellation. But before you buy one, experiment with what you have and see if you're happy with the results.

SOFTWARE

Conveniently enough, all the applications and utilities I use to create podcasts are free. Here's what they are and where you can download them.

PLATFORM
- ■ Windows
- ■ Macintosh
- ■ Linux

FUNCTION	SOFTWARE	Windows	Macintosh	Linux	WHERE TO FIND IT
Telephony	Skype	■	■	■	*skype.com*
	iChat/AIM	■	■		*apple.com / aol.com*
Audio Stream Routing	VAC	■			*ntonyx.com/vac.htm*
	Soundflower		■		*cycling74.com/products/soundflower.html*
	Soundflowerbed (optional)		■		*cycling74.com/products/soundflower.html*
	LineIn		■		*rogueamoeba.com/freebies*
	AudioHijack Pro (optional)		■		*rogueamoeba.com/audiohijackpro*
Audio Recording / Mixing	Audacity	■	■	■	*audacity.sourceforge.net*
	GarageBand		■		*apple.com*
Encoding	LameLib		■		*spaghetticode.org/lame*
	LAME	■			*mitiok.free.fr*
Podcast Receiving (called a podder or podcatcher)	iPodder	■	■	■	*ipodder.sourceforge.net*
	Other apps at *ipodder.org/ directory/4/ipodderSoftware*				

MAKE IT.

PODCAST PRODUCTION STEP-BY-STEP

START ⟩⟩   Time: **An Afternoon** Complexity: **Low**

1. RECORD YOUR MATERIAL

RECORDING IN PERSON

On a laptop. If you're just recording yourself or conducting an in-person interview, you can use a laptop and a microphone. You'll need an audio application. If you already have one you like, then great — stick with that. Otherwise, I recommend Audacity, a free, open source, cross-platform audio recording and editing tool. Download Audacity and take some time to familiarize yourself with it. Try recording and importing WAV and MP3 files, and cutting and pasting sections around. Also, see if you like how your microphone sounds.

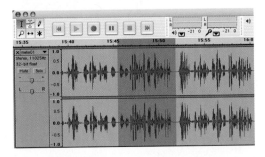

On a portable device. On the street, an iPod or other small recording device is an even more portable way to capture in-person interviews. I've recorded audio on my iPod using Podzilla (see *Mod Your Pod*, page 135) and using Griffin's iTalk accessory. If you're an old pro, you're probably already sporting a MiniDisc recorder.

RECORDING REMOTELY OVER SKYPE OR ICHAT

Using Skype. This free internet telephony application is a great way to conduct remote interviews and conference calls for podcasting (and I use it now for most of my regular phone calls as well). Download, install, and sign into Skype. If your interviewee has done the same, the call is free; otherwise you can pay 2 cents per minute to call their regular phone, anywhere in the world.

Using iChat. On the Mac, you can use iChat instead of Skype, but it only supports conference calls in Mac OS 10.4 (Tiger) and above.

Route the output. Now we need to route Skype or iChat's audio output into our recording application, Audacity. Unfortunately, operating systems still have a hard time routing audio between applications, so we'll need to chain them together with a hodgepodge of platform-specific utilities. Given the variety in sound setups, sound cards, input devices, and recording applications, be prepared for a little trial and error.

SOUND QUALITY VS. FILE SIZE

I record most things at 44 kHz, 16-bit stereo, but you can choose lower or higher quality to reduce file size or improve the sound. If you think you might want to save your audio to CD or another "audiophile" format later, record at a higher quality; you can always compress or convert it later.

Skype/iChat recording on the Mac.
1. Download and install Soundflower and LineIn.
Restart after installation. Optionally, you can also download and install Soundflowerbed, which adds a handy menu item for quick switching.

2. Open System Preferences/Sound. Set Output to Playback and Input to your microphone or headset.

3. Launch Skype. In Preferences/Audio, set Audio Output to Soundflower (2ch) and Audio Input to your microphone or headset.

4. Launch LineIn. Set Input From and Output to your recording app (e.g. Audacity). Then click Pass Thru.

5. Call Echo123, Skype's testing service, and make sure you hear the test message and your own voice through the speaker.

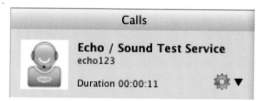

6. Launch Audacity. Under Preferences/Audio I/O, choose Soundflower (2ch) for both Playback and Recording Device.

7. Call (or continue talking to) Echo123 in Skype, and start recording in Audacity. If everything works, you'll capture all the audio.

Troubleshooting
Some applications need to be launched before others in order to communicate. Unfortunately, this can vary from system to system. So if this Skype — LineIn — Audacity order doesn't work, exit them all and try some launch order variations.

Other Things to Try:
Route through Soundflower (16ch), not (2ch).
Try another audio application, like GarageBand.
Try another routing app, like AudioHijack Pro (or its free demo version).
Conference call via a PC logged into a third Skype account and use the PC for recording. A bit clunky and using a PC to help a Mac, but it sometimes works.

Skype recording on Windows.
On the PC (Windows XP), we're also going to use Skype and Audacity. See the *On the laptop* section (previous page) for Audacity setup (it's the same for PC and Mac). What's different is how to configure Skype and route its audio. Note that the recipe below, which uses XP's Control Panel/Sound Properties window, works for many systems. But with the PC's zillion possible configurations, sound cards, and audio drivers, your mileage may vary.

1. Launch Skype and Audacity.

2. Open XP's Volume Control Properties by double-clicking the volume icon on the task bar.

3. Call Echo123, the Skype testing service.

4. Click Playback and select Microphone in Volume Control/Options. Raise microphone level and click OK. Then click Recording and select Stereo Mix.

Troubleshooting
Try switching the settings before or during a call, and watch the sound input levels in Audacity to detect when the sound is being routed. You can also use VAC (Virtual Audio Cable), which routes audio from all your devices to Audacity or other sound applications. Check out Virtual Audio Cable at spider.nrcde.ru/music/software/eng/vac.html.

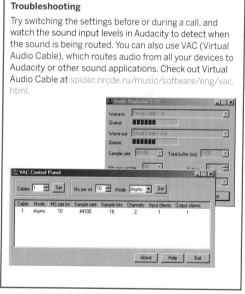

2. EDIT THE PODCAST

Once you have your recording, you may want to edit out gaps, remove umms and hmms, and add music or effects. Sound editing is more art than science, and the best way to make a podcast omelet is to break some eggs. Now is also the time to add intro and outro material.

If your interview, music, and other sounds are of different volumes, you should adjust them to even things out. You can do this quickly in Audacity by selecting Edit/Select All and then Effects/Normalize.

Todd Cochrane's weekly podcasts cover DRM crackery and other topics that fascinate geeks and are indecipherable to others. *geeknewscentral.com.*

3. COMPRESS THE FILE

Editing and exporting audio on the Mac.
Audacity doesn't come with an MP3 converter, because MP3 conversion software can't legally be distributed in free programs. But Audacity and other audio applications can plug in third-party encoders such as LAME.

3a. Download an MP3 codec library, if you haven't already, that works on your platform (see software chart) and extract it to your Audacity folder. Within Audacity, open Preferences/File Format, choose Find Library, and point to the converter. Now you'll be able to save MP3s.

3b. Choose your bit rate in Audacity Preferences/File Format. For voice, I generally use 32 kbps with a sample rate of 22kHz. For a 30-minute segment, I try to keep the files less than 8 megabytes. Experiment with different settings, and keep in mind that many listeners use phones and other devices without much space.

3c. Export your file (or files). Within Audacity, select File/Export as MP3 and/or Export as Ogg. If your audio application can only save WAV files, create the WAV, then use another application to convert via Import/Save As. When Audacity exports an MP3, it will prompt you to fill out the tag information. I usually leave it blank and add this later (see step 4).

4. TAG AND PACKAGE THE FILE

4a. Name the file. You can name your file anything (provided you keep the proper extension), but it's considerate to follow a convention that helps listeners find shows in their podcast collections:

Show_title-year-month-day.file_extension

For example, the MP3 version of MAKE: Audio's June 1, 2005, show would be:

MAKE-2005-06-01.mp3

4b. Choose a CC license. A Creative Commons license is a more flexible copyright (a "copyleft") that lets you retain some rights to your works but also encourages sharing, which is what makes podcasts so popular. You can choose a license and find out more at creativecommons.org. For MAKE: Audio, we permit copying and distribution, but only for non-commercial purposes and with credit given, and we prohibit derivative works without permission. This license can be found at creativecommons.org/licenses/by-nc-nd/2.0.

4c. Tag the file. MP3s contain metadata text that you can add to files, such as Song title, Artist, and Genre. Not all players will show these tags, but they're good to add. You can tag an MP3 using many methods, but I use iTunes. To do this, drag the file into the iTunes panel, and then select it and choose File/Get Info. Click the Info tab, and enter the information you want to include. For Comments, you're limited to around 250 characters. I generally list who is on the show, what it's about, and the Creative Commons license. "Podcast" isn't listed in the Genre, but I type it in.

4d. Add artwork (optional). The MP3 format also supports an Artwork tag, which can contain any images you want to include. Most portable players won't display these, but they'll show up in desktop players and on the new color-screen iPod. Adding art increases the file size, however, so you should keep it down to a single JPG or GIF image, 320x240 or smaller. In iTunes, the Artwork tab on the Get Info window you just opened lets you add and delete images.

Doug Kaye's IT Conversations podcast visits top conferences and talks to leading minds about RSS (of course), the impact of technology on social networks, and other issues. You could spend a good month with his material so far, and it's directly listener-supported — so if you like what you hear, please contribute to the tip jar. *itconversations.com.*

TIPS FOR GOOD INTERVIEWS

Prepare to be spontaneous. The best way to ensure you'll feel free and conversational is to do your homework. Know the story and what you want to ask the person on the other end of your mic.

Show, don't tell. Think cinema. In dialogue with your subject, and in gathering ambient sound to accompany the piece, think of your podcast as a movie.

Don't condescend to your audience. When framing your questions or editing, avoid making assumptions about what your listener already knows.

Don't condescend to your interviewee. You're there because you don't know the answers, so don't assume that you know the subject's position or opinion. Enter the dialogue with a sense of respectful curiosity. It's your job to unearth insight, and an understanding of who this person is, for strangers who wouldn't otherwise get the chance.

Push. If you can't reach an answer you need one way, try a different route. Ease into the tougher stuff. Everyone wants to be understood; is there something your subject would like the world to understand that has been botched or missed before?

—Xeni Jardin

5. PUBLISH AND SYNDICATE YOUR PODCAST

5a. Upload the file. At this point, I usually drag the file back out of iTunes to my desktop, and then upload it to my server via FTP. If the show becomes popular, you'll need a server that can handle the traffic, but hosting generally isn't free.

Some podcasters share the load with BitTorrent (bittorent.com), which is free but not easy to install. Others use Apple's .Mac service, but they've been known to shut off too-popular files. This is a topic we discuss on makezine.com. The important thing is to upload the file to any public server space with a URL you can link to.

5b. Create and publish the RSS feed. The magic of podcasting happens when a podcatcher checks an RSS feed to see if there's a new show. If so, it downloads the show for you to play later. Blogging applications like Movable Type have plug-ins that automatically create an RSS feed, so if you use one of these, it's worth checking for this.

Otherwise, here's how you can roll your own in any text or HTML editor. Create a file that looks as shown below (the blue parts are what you change every time you publish a new podcast; the black text is an RSS template):

```
<?xml version="1.0" encoding="iso-8859-1"?>
  <rss version="2.0">
  <channel>
  <title>Title of your site</title>
  <link>http://www.yourserver/podcast_info_page/</link>
  <description>All about your Podcast</description>
  <language>en-us</language>
  <lastBuildDate>Fri, 01 Jun 2005 08:00:00 +0000</last
  BuildDate>
  <pubDate>Fri, 01 Jun 2005 08:00:00 +0000</pubDate>
  <item>
  <title>Title of your podcast.</title>
  <description>Show notes and other information.</description>
  <enclosure url="http://www.yourserver.com/yourfile.
  mp3" length="31337707" type="audio/mpeg"/>
  </item>
  </channel>
  </rss>
```

In the enclosure tag, the URL value is the server location of the file; length is the file size in bytes; and type is the file type and format. Other possible enclosure type values include application/ogg (for Ogg Vorbis), video/mpg, video/quicktime, image/ jpg, and application/x-bittorrent. You can learn more RSS capabilities at blogs.law.harvard.edu/tech/rss. lastBuild and pubDate are the times the feed was last updated and published (for us, the same thing). It's important to keep these up-to-date so pod-catcher applications know when you've published something new.

Save this file, in plain text format, with the exten-sion "xml" (for example, **podcast.xml**). Then upload this file to your server. This is the file that tells the podcatcher apps what you have to offer, and you'll update it with another <item> section whenever you publish a new podcast.

5c. Create OPML show notes (optional). Outline Processor Markup Language (OPML) is an HTML/ XML relative that's used to create outlines. Some podcasters create notes for their shows in OPML format and upload them alongside the XML, making a richer layer of documentation available to compat-ible podcatchers. While not a requirement, it's worth checking out at opml.org.

5d. Publish to the web. You're almost a podcaster! Now you need to let the world know about your podcast. There are a few directory sites you can register your podcast on, with more in the works. Start by filling out the forms at audio.weblogs.com, podcastalley.com, and odeo.com.

You've recorded your audio, edited it, compressed, tagged, uploaded, syndicated, and published it. You're a podcaster now. Talk hard — and welcome to the revolution!

CREATE A MUSICAL INTRO WITH GARAGEBAND

If you use GarageBand, you can use the loop browser to create music for your podcasts. I dragged-and-dropped the bongo drum intro for MAKE: Audio from Garage-Band right into the Audacity track. *Voilà*, a free and easy orchestra.

USE IT.

FINDING YOUR VOICE (AND OTHERS)

BUILDING AN AUDIENCE

The most important part of all comes next: building an audience. Tell people about your podcasts. Participate in the forums on podcast sites. Listen to any audience feedback you receive, and use it to make your podcasts better.

But the surest way you'll develop an audience is through your material. My best advice is to follow the things you're passionate about. If you have a good show and you keep it fresh, people will find you.

FINDING OTHER PODCASTS

The types of podcasts out there are as varied as the web itself. The majority of podcasts tend to be bloggers who use the audio medium to supplement their sites. Podcasts aren't censored, they're not bound by any time limit, and there are no rules.

To get an idea of the more popular podcasts out there, check out my favorite spot: Podcast Alley at podcastalley.com.

You can also see the latest podcasts published from all over the web on audio.weblogs.com. When a podcast is published, the site is usually notified (pinged) and populates the list. If you're ready to listen to your first podcast, then it's now time to grab an application that will do the podcast grabbing for you.

LISTENING TO OTHER PODCASTS

Browse and search podcasts on the same sites where you published yours. Of these, my favorite again is Podcast Alley, which features forums and vote-based rankings.

On the application side, dozens of podder/pod-catcher "getters" have been coming out, and most of the ones I've tried work just fine. iPodder.org is a great resource for assessing what's available. My favorite is the iPodder, the standard, which is free, cross-platform, supports BitTorrent, and lets you

add podcast feeds from the iPodder.org directory without having to manually cut and paste them in.

Podcasting can be used for any type of file, not just audio. Following the usual succession of tech capabilities, video podcasting (a.k.a. videocasting) is starting to pick up steam, and we'll explain how to do it in the future.

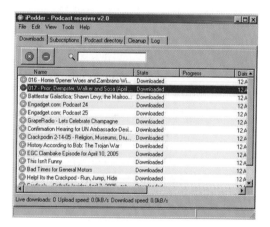

The Dawn and Drew Show is a hysterical, unscripted quad-weekly podcast from a married couple who live in a Wisconsin farmhouse. *dawnanddrew.com*

MOUSEY THE JUNKBOT

By Gareth Branwyn

With a few spare parts, you can turn an old computer mouse into an amusing little robot. >>

Set up: p.99   **Make it:** p.100   **Use it:** p.109

THE FINE ART OF MAKING "FRANKENMICE"

This project turns an analog computer mouse into a robot that'll delight friends and wow workmates down on the cube farm. Mousey's behavior is fittingly mouse-like. It scoots quickly across the floor, thanks to lively little motors. And when the critter crashes into anything, it speeds off in the opposite direction.

The robot's "brains" are an ingenious hack based on an audio operational amplifier (op-amp), an 8-pin chip that's normally used to drive answering machine speakers and other lo-fi equipment. Following Randy Sargent's pioneering design (see page 102), Mousey repurposes this chip to boost light-sensor input to motor-powerable levels. The result is simple, fast-reacting analog circuitry that fits inside a mouse case.

Gareth Branwyn writes about the intersection of technology and culture for *Wired* and other publications, and is a member of MAKE's Advisory Board. He is also "Cyborg-in-Chief" of *Streettech.com*.

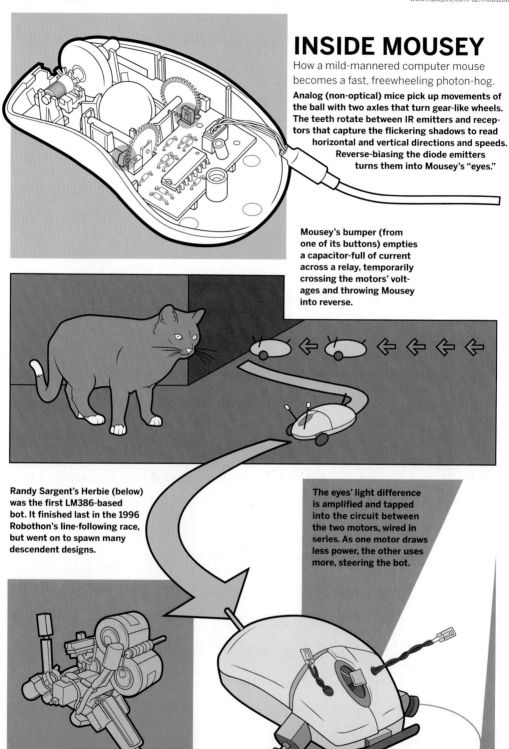

INSIDE MOUSEY

How a mild-mannered computer mouse becomes a fast, freewheeling photon-hog.

Analog (non-optical) mice pick up movements of the ball with two axles that turn gear-like wheels. The teeth rotate between IR emitters and receptors that capture the flickering shadows to read horizontal and vertical directions and speeds. Reverse-biasing the diode emitters turns them into Mousey's "eyes."

Mousey's bumper (from one of its buttons) empties a capacitor-full of current across a relay, temporarily crossing the motors' voltages and throwing Mousey into reverse.

Randy Sargent's Herbie (below) was the first LM386-based bot. It finished last in the 1996 Robothon's line-following race, but went on to spawn many descendent designs.

The eyes' light difference is amplified and tapped into the circuit between the two motors, wired in series. As one motor draws less power, the other uses more, steering the bot.

Illustration by Timmy Kucynda

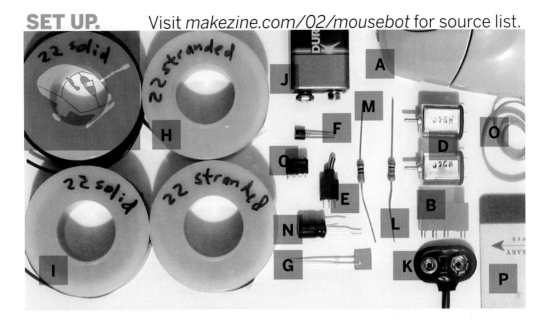

First, you'll need an analog (non-optical) mouse to cannibalize for its case and several parts inside. If you don't have an old mouse or two gathering dust, ask friends and colleagues. Otherwise, you can buy a new, super-cheap model such as the Kensington ValueMouse, which costs $10 and has enough space to fit all of your components inside. The bigger and more symmetrical the mouse, the easier the build will be. "Handed" mice with asymmetrical, curved bodies present problems.

The other components can be scavenged, or purchased from an electronics retailer. For the motors and other specialty parts, we recommend Dave Hrynkiw's Solarbotics (solarbotics.com) as an excellent source. Where available, we've listed Solarbotics parts numbers for components, and they now offer a complete mousey kit for about $20 (without the mouse).

For an electronic symbols key, see page 113.

MATERIALS:

Mouse case [A]

2 Light sensors
From mouse

SPST touch switch
From mouse

Double-pole, double-throw (DPDT) 5-volt relay [B]
From analog modem, or Solarbotics #RE1

LM386 audio operational amplifier (op-amp) [C]
From answering machine, speakerphone, intercom, etc., or Solarbotics #LM386

2 Small 4.5 VDC motors [D] From motorized toys, or Solarbotics #RM1A / Mabu-chi FF-030-PN

SPST toggle switch [E]
Solarbotics #SWT2

2N3904 or PN2222 NPN-type transistor [F]
Solarbotics #TR3904/ TR2222

Light-emitting diode (LED) [G]

2 Spools of 22 to 24-gauge stranded hook-up wire [H]
Ideally, 1 black and 1 red

4 Pieces of 22-gauge, solid-core hook-up wire [I]
Ideally, 2 red and 2 black, 6½" long

9V battery [J]

9V battery snap [K]

1kΩ to 20kΩ resistor [L]

1kΩ resistor [M]

10µF to 100µF electrolytic capacitor [N]

Rubber band or other tire-making material [O]

Small piece of plastic [P]
At least ¼" x 2½" of hard, springy, thin plastic, like .030" Plasticard stock, or an old credit card

Piece of Velcro or two-way tape (optional)

TOOLS:

Phillips screwdriver
For disassembling mouse

Dremel tool
With bits and cutting discs

Needlenose pliers

Digital multimeter (DMM)

X-ACTO/hobby knife

Soldering iron

Solder sucker or desoldering bulb

Wire cutters/wire snips

Breadboard, hook-up wire

Superglue, epoxy, or other contact cement

Poster putty, electrical tape, cellophane tape

Ruler

Protective goggles, mask

MAKE IT.

BUILD YOUR ROBOT MOUSE

START >>

Time: **A Day** Complexity: **Medium**

1. MOUSEY'S CIRCUITRY IS FREEFORMED

This means that we'll solder the parts to each other without a circuit board, building everything up right inside the mouse case. But before we do this, we'll need to prep the case and install the motors, and then breadboard the circuitry separately to make sure everything works.

Before unholstering your Dremel tool, you'll need to determine if the mouse has enough space inside. Unscrew the mouse case and eyeball it to make sure that it will hold the two DC motors and a 9-volt battery. Screws may be hiding under little nylon feet or tape strips on the bottom of the mouse. Save these bits so you can put them back at the end of the build; they'll help reduce friction.

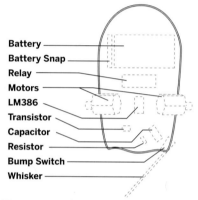

Battery
Battery Snap
Relay
Motors
LM386
Transistor
Capacitor
Resistor
Bump Switch
Whisker

Mouse case and parts that need to fit inside.

Cleared-out mouse case.

2. PERFORM AN ALIEN MOUSE AUTOPSY

Once you have a suitable candidate, remove all of the mechanics and electronics. Unhook the mouse cable from its plug-type connector, pop out the scroll wheel (if it has one), and then pry out the PCB (printed circuit board). Set these parts aside. Then use your Dremel and cut-off wheel to hollow out the case, removing all of the plastic mounts and partitions inside, except for any screw post(s) that hold the case together. Do the same for the top half, although you may want to leave the mounts that hold the buttons in place.

Note: Plastic dust is nasty stuff, so work on newspaper and wear goggles and a mask.

3. ADD THE POWER SWITCH

The last piece of preparatory bodywork is adding the power switch, a large toggle placed rear topside so it looks like a tail. Find an appropriate mouse-tail location, then drill a hole in the case big enough for the switch. If the switch has a threaded bushing and two nuts, take one nut off, insert the bushing up through the hole, and then tighten the nut back down onto the outside of the case. In some cases, a plastic screw post interferes with the tail area. If so, you can cut out the post and reconnect the top and bottom halves with tape or glue.

The top of our mouse case with its toggle "tail" installed.

Illustrations by Mark Frauenfelder

4. MOTOR AND BATTERY PLACEMENT

Now we're ready to figure out the arrangement of the bigger components and cut openings for the motors. Mouse shapes vary, so you'll use some judgment here, but the two motors should be oriented perpendicular to the centerline of the body, so the bot travels in a straight line. Also be sure to leave enough space behind the motors for the battery.

Once you've placed the motors and battery, you're ready to cut openings for the axles and wheels, which are simply the drive shafts and gears of the motors.

You'll want to angle the shafts coming out of the mouse body so they support the bot and set a proper speed. The steeper the angle, the less rubber will meet the road, which slows the bot down – but this is good, since many builders have complained that Mousey moves too fast. If you're using the lively Solarbotics RM1 motors, 60 degrees is about right, as shown.

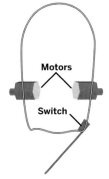

Motors

Switch

Eventual whisker

Motor placement, angle, and switch placement are very important for making Mousey work properly.

Use poster putty to hold the motors in place temporarily. Then get down at eye level and make sure the gear "wheels" are making good, level contact with the table. Once the motors are positioned properly, glue them in place.

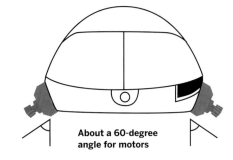

About a 60-degree angle for motors

5. MAKE THE BUMP SWITCH AND TIRES

Your mousebot will have a giant "whisker" – a bump switch (courtesy of one of the mouse's button switches) that triggers Mousey's scuttle-away behavior. Look on the mouse PCB (see photo in Step 7) for a tiny plastic box that clicks when

Finished motor and bump switch installation. Shown with battery test fit.

you press it down; then desolder it. Once you have the switch removed, attach the base with putty to one side of your mouse's front end. Tape the strip of hard plastic in place, so that it covers the tiny switch button and runs along the front of the mouse like a wide bumper. The idea is to have the switch triggered by a bump anywhere along the length of the "whisker," so when you press in the plastic, you should hear an itty-bitty click. Tweak this arrangement until it looks good. Once you have your placement, drill a small opening in the mouse case bottom for the switch to stick out. Also cut the plastic strip down to size, about ¼" x 2½".

The last mechanical modification needed for the bottom half is adding tires. Find a rubber band with the same width as the sprockets on the drive shafts, and then cut it to length, wrap it around, and glue it on. You can make the wheels thicker by continuing to wrap the band around itself. Rubber or plastic tubing also makes good tires, as does corrugated tubing from a Lego Mindstorms robot kit or the rubber cylinders from Dremel drum sander bits.

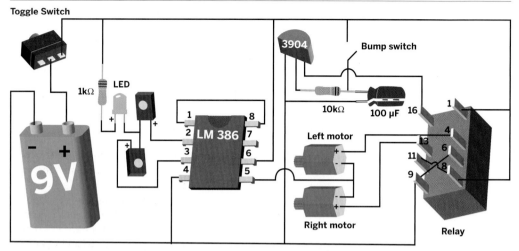

6. UNDERSTAND MOUSEY'S BRAIN

The LM386 op-amp, the main component of Mousey's control circuit, "listens" to two input signals. If one signal is lower than the other, the chip boosts that signal to equalize the one output. In our case, the inputs are light values rather than audio. If we hook this output to two DC motors, we have a little brain that reads input from two light sensors, compares them, and boosts the power on the dimmer side. This creates a robot that follows a light source, auto-correcting itself as it moves.

The bump switch triggers a relay that reverses the two motors' inputs for a few seconds. This makes Mousey scuttle away from light after any collision, adding to its lifelike behavior. The diagram above shows the circuit diagram for Mousey's brain.

Use this diagram as a reference as you build your mousebot.

A larger version of this image can be found at http://xrl.us/fkxi.

BEAM ROBOTICS: SURVIVAL OF THE FUNNEST

Mousey comes out of the BEAM design tradition, a biology-inspired doctrine which frowns on microprocessors in favor of simple analog control, in order to create robots that act and react with the physical world directly, perhaps instinctively.

BEAM's natural selection process occurs at conventions and gatherings like Robothon, where bots compete against one another in races, "sumo" matches, high jumps, rope climbs, and other Olympics-style events.

Through BEAM's 14 years of evolution, BEAMers worldwide have designed and refined numerous species of inexpensive and easy-to-build robo-critters, including photovores such as Mousey, four- and six-legged walkers, sun-powered solarollers, and swimming aquavores.

Mousey's circuitry is based on Randy Sargent's line-follower bot Herbie, which competed in the Seattle Robothon in 1996. Many variations of the design followed,

including Dave Hrynkiw's Herbie Photovore. Following Dave's example, we built ours with as much techno-junk as possible, including an old computer mouse and a 5-volt double-pole, double-throw (DPDT) relay – a component found inside most analog modems.

BEAM Resources
The acronym BEAM stands for "Biology, Electronics, Aesthetics, and Mechanics" and was coined by Mark Tilden.

Solarbotics: The main BEAM portal Solarbotics.net

Yahoo! Groups: BEAM Robotics
groups.yahoo.com/group/beam

Robothon: Seattle, Oct. 8-9, 2005
robothon.com

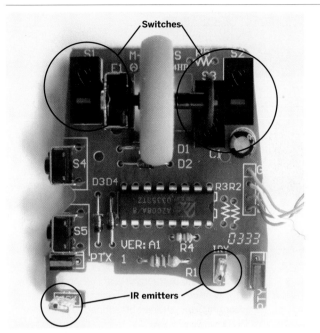

Switches

D1

D2

D3D4

R3R2

VER: A1

PTX 1

R4

R1

IR emitters

A pair of IR emitters will serve as your robot's eyes. Note their likely location on the mouse's PCB.

7. CREATE MOUSEY'S EYES

For Mousey's eyes, we can use the mouse's own two IR emitters, a.k.a. phototransistors. During normal computer mousing, these shine infrared through the mouse's perforated encoder wheels, which is then received by photodetectors on the other side.

Like many fundamental devices, these emitters can work as both transmitters and receivers. As receivers, they're more robust and less specialized than the mouse's dedicated internal photoreceivers, and this makes them a better choice for Mousey's eyes to the outside world. On most mice, the emitters are clear plastic boxes with a tiny dome protruding from one face, while the detectors are solid black.

Find the clear emitters and desolder them from the PCB. You are now the proud owner of a pair of robot eyeballs.

8. GIVE MOUSEY EYESTALKS

Our IR emitters only have two stubby little pins coming out. We need to give Mousey some optic nerves – eyestalks that jut from the front of its body. These not only look cool, but also allow you to adjust Mousey's sensitivity to light by bending the stalks around.

First we need to determine which pin on each emitter is positive and which is negative. Set your digital multimeter to Diode Check mode, and touch the probes to each pin. If the read-out is "OL" (no connection), reverse the probes. When connected correctly, you should get a reading of about 1V, with the red probe indicating the anode (or positive) pin. If your DMM doesn't have Diode Check, look for a positive voltage of about 0.6V when the red probe is on the anode.

To create the stalks, cut four 6½" pieces of 22-gauge, solid-core hook-up wire. If you have red and black, cut two of each color. Solid core is better than stranded in this case, because it makes stiffer stalks

Our finished eyestalks, ready to shed some light on our control circuit.

that hold their shape when you mold them.

Solder the red wire to the cathode (-) pins on the emitters and the black wires to the anode (+) pins. The colors are switched because we're reverse-biasing the diodes; with current flowing in the normal direction, additional electrons excited by light in the diode's junction get lost in the flow, but with current trickling the opposite way, the difference is more noticeable, making the circuit more sensitive. When the wires are soldered in place, twist them together and strip some of the jacket off of the other ends.

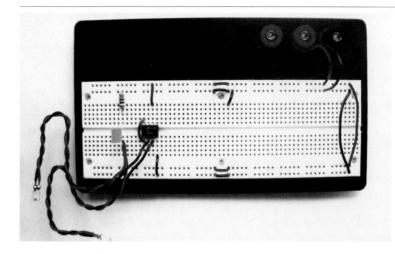

The first part of Mousey's brain: sensors and main control circuit.

9. HOOK UP THE OP-AMP

With all of your electronic components in hand, we're ready to breadboard. Here are the steps to install the op-amp chip and main control circuit:

9a. Install the LM386 chip across the trench on your breadboard. With all ICs, pins are numbered counter-clockwise around, starting at the little dimple.

9b. Connect tie-points for Pins 1 and 8 together with a piece of hook-up wire. These two pins control the op-amp's gain; by connecting them with a jumper, we're increasing the circuit's sensitivity to the input.

9c. Connect the eyestalks by taking the black wires from each and connecting them to tie points for Pins 2 and 3 (the op-amp's inputs). Connect the red wires together by plugging them into a node about

five or six rows left of the chip. Our horizontally oriented board is organized with +/- power supply at top/bottom and all chips facing left. Translate accordingly for different breadboard layouts.

9d. Plug the negative lead of an LED (the shorter end) into the node with the two red eyestalk wires, and the positive lead into a new node on the opposite side of the trench. Then take a 1k-ohm resistor and plug one end into the LED's positive node, and the other end into the positive/upper power bus. These components constitute a sensitivity-boosting subcircuit originally developed by Wilf Rigter.

9e. Finish this part of your circuit by connecting the power pin of the LM386 (Pin 6) to the positive power bus, and the ground (Pin 4) to the lower/negative bus. We'll connect the battery later.

10. CREATE THE RUNAWAY CIRCUIT

If we hooked up Mousey's motors and battery at this point, it would simply chase a light source. Now we'll make it more interesting by adding Mousey's whisker-triggered "fear" reflex. To create the runaway circuit, we need the bump switch you already pulled, a 5V DPDT relay, a transistor, and a simple timer consisting of a capacitor and a resistor. When the switch is triggered, the transistor enables the runaway circuit, where the capacitor powers Mousey's motors in reverse. When the capacitor has fully discharged a few seconds later, the transistor switches motor control back to the regular, light-following circuit.

The resistance and capacitance determine the rate and amount of current discharged, and you can play with different resistor and cap values until you find the runaway behavior you want. Try resistors in the 1k- to 20k-ohm range, and capacitors in the 10- to 100-microfarad range. With both, the higher the value, the longer the discharge time. We used a 10k-ohm resistor and a 100-microfarad capacitor, which gave about 8 seconds of fast backing up. Here are the steps for breadboarding the runaway circuit:

10a. The relay's pins are spaced apart widely, so we'll refer to pins by their breadboard locations. Plug in the relay about six nodes to the right of the LM386, or 1-16 (although the relay actually has only eight pins).

10b. Cross a wire from Pin 8 to Pin 11 and another from Pin 6 to Pin 9. These two wires will reverse the motor connections when the relay is engaged.

10c. Plug the capacitor's positive lead into an unused row just left of the relay, and the cathode to the negative power bus. On electrolytic caps, the cathode is usually marked with a stripe or (-) symbol.

10d. Plug in one end of the higher-ohm resistor to connect with the capacitor anode, and jump the other end over the trench to a new node on the other side.

10e. Spread the transistor's pins and plug it in with the flat side facing the trench, above the relay, such that the center pin (base) connects to the resistor lead, the left pin (emitter) is in an unused node, and the right pin (collector) connects to Pin 16 of the relay.

10f. Plug one hook-up wire into the bottom resistor and capacitor node, somewhere between the two, and a second wire up to the positive power bus. Bend the tips of the wires so they can touch, but keep them separated. These wires will act as the

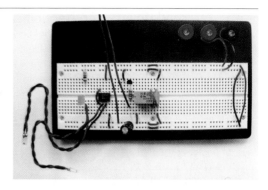

Our breadboard with control chip, timer, and relay circuits installed.

bump switch when you touch them together. We're being lazy and assuming that the switch works, but you can hook the wires up to it to make sure.

10g. Run two wires to connect Pin 1 and Pin 8 on the relay with the top/positive power bus. Connect Pin 9 to the negative bus. Finally, connect the transistor's left pin (emitter) to the bottom/negative bus. This connects the relay and transistor to power. That's it — look over your cool robot brain!

11. CONNECT THE MOTORS AND POWER

Now we're ready to connect the motors and power and see if it all works. Take the right motor and connect its negative terminal to Pin 5 of the LM386 chip and its positive terminal to Pin 13 on the relay. Take the left motor and connect its negative to Pin 5 of the chip, and positive to Pin 4 on the relay. On many motors, the positive terminal is marked with a dimple or a (+) symbol.

Finally, connect the 9V battery to the board via a battery snap or clips, recalling that the battery's "outie" snap is its negative pole. Your breadboard should look like the image at right, and the motors should run. If so, congratulations! Get yourself a flashlight and start having fun moving the beam around Mousey's light sensors, noticing the speed changes. Then touch the switch wires together, hear the relay click, and see the motors reverse their direction.

If all did not go well, check that everything's where it should be, with the capacitor, resistors, and transistor in the proper holes and power running in the right direction. Some breadboards split their power

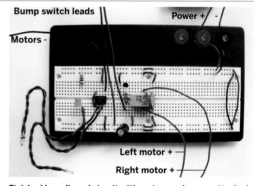

Bump switch leads   Power + -
Motors -
Left motor +
Right motor +

Finished breadboard circuit with motors and power attached.

busses into multiple segments; in this case, you need to connect the battery to each occupied segment of the power bus, or else wire them together. Use a fresh battery, and probe around with the multimeter to make sure that the right amount of power is getting where it should. If the eyes don't work, check the eyestalk solder joins, and if necessary, swap the eyeballs out for another set from another old mouse. Some definitely work better than others.

12. FREEFORM MOUSEY'S CONTROL CIRCUIT

Now that we have a light-hungry robot brain, we need to install it in our mouse body so that it can feed (cue *Night of the Living Dead* sound effects here). In general, we'll want to use a lighter wire, such as stranded 22-gauge, to tuck into the case and put less stress on the solder joints.

Before soldering, test fit all the parts inside your case, starting with the battery, motors, and bump switch. Then position the other components around these. The resistor/LED sensitivity-booster circuit will fit against the top half. As you arrange, check that the case still closes, and leave some headroom for the wires. When you're happy with your arrangement, empty the case and install the battery using two-way tape, Velcro tape, or poster putty. That way, you can replace it when Mousey gets that run-down feeling.

13. INSTALL THE RELAY

To prepare the relay for installation, put it in "dead bug mode" (on its back), and solder short lengths of solid-core wire to the bottom four pins (the switch pins) in an X configuration, as shown.

13a. Solder the transistor's collector (the right pin when you're looking at the flat side with the pins pointing down) to the top-left coil pin on the relay, Pin 16 on the breadboard. Solder a 4" piece of black wire (denoting negative) to the transistor's emitter. This will connect to Pin 4 of the IC and negative power.

13b. Solder a short red wire connecting the top and bottom pins on the relay's right side, Pins 1 and 8. Solder a 2" black (negative) wire onto the bottom-left pin, Pin 9, and then a 3" red wire onto the bottom-right, Pin 8.

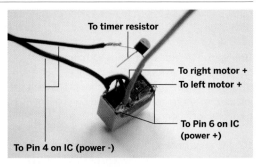

13c. Glue the relay into the case, in dead bug mode, and allow it to dry before soldering anything else to it. We glued ours between the motors.

13d. Using red wire, solder the left motor's positive terminal to the second pin down on the right side (Pin 4 on the breadboard), and solder the right motor's positive to the opposite pin on the relay, Pin 13.

14. CONNECT THE SWITCH COMPONENTS

With the relay close to the front, we can chain together the timer resistor, capacitor, and bump switch without needing additional wires. As with the relay, we'll attach components "out of body" first, for easier soldering.

14a. Solder a 4" black wire to the capacitor's negative lead (which should be marked).

14b. Using a multimeter on your 3-pin bump switch, determine which side pin connects with the middle pin when you click, and clip off the other side pin.

14c. Solder the cap's positive lead to the remaining side pin of the bump switch, and solder one end of the timer resistor to the same pole.

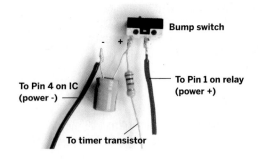

14d. Solder a 2" red lead to the middle bump switch pin, and then glue the switch into the body, through the hole you cut earlier.

14e. Solder a lead between the transistor's middle pin and the free end of the timer resistor.

15. POWER TO THE MOTORS

15a. Solder two 2" black wires to the motors' negative terminals, then solder the stripped ends of these two wires together side-by-side.

15b. Solder a third, 3" black wire to these joined ends, then solder it to the control chip's output pin (Pin 5).

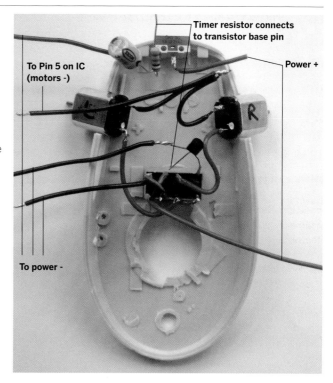

To Pin 5 on IC (motors -)

Timer resistor connects to transistor base pin

Power +

To power -

16. INSTALL THE LM386 CONTROL CHIP

16a. Bend Pins 1 and 8 of the op-amp chip down and solder them together.

16b. Find the black wires from the transistor, the relay, and the capacitor, strip the ends, and solder them all together side-by-side.

16c. Solder the battery snap's negative wire to this same junction.

16d. Solder a 1" black wire to Pin 4 of the op-amp, and the other end to the negative wire junction.

16e. Solder the red wire from the relay to Pin 6 of the chip. Then glue the chip into the mouse case in dead bug mode.

That's it for Mousey's bottom half!

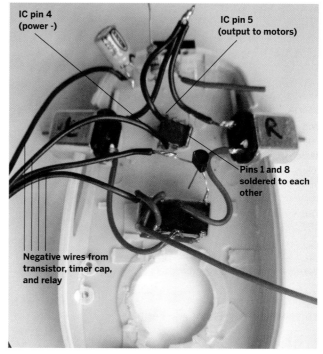

IC pin 4 (power -)

IC pin 5 (output to motors)

Pins 1 and 8 soldered to each other

Negative wires from transistor, timer cap, and relay

The LM386 control chip wired and ready for action.

17. INSTALL MOUSEY'S EYES

17a. The buttons on most computer mice are separate, semi-attached pieces of plastic. To give Mousey's eyes a solid foundation, glue the buttons down, wait until dry, and then drill small holes in Mousey's lid to thread the eyestalks through.

17b. Thread about 1¾" of stalk through each hole. On the inside, trim the two red wires so that they just overlap against the underside of the lid, then solder them together. Run the black wires back along the inside and bend them down where the op-amp is located (but don't solder them yet).

17c. Make the sensitivity booster circuit by cutting a 1" piece of red wire, and soldering one end to the 1k-ohm resistor and the other end to the LED's anode.

17d. Connect the booster by soldering the free end of the resistor to the middle pole of the toggle switch and the LED cathode to the junction of the two red eyestalk wires.

17e. Mark where the LED sits, gently bend it aside,

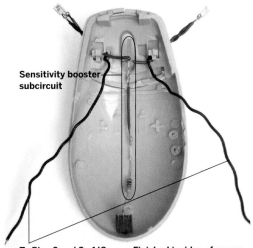

Sensitivity booster subcircuit

To Pins 2 and 3 of IC

Finished insides of mouse top with eyestalk placement, sensitivity booster, and power switch.

and drill a hole in the case for the LED to poke out of (unless it can already come up through the scroll wheel slot). Push the LED through and hold it in place with electrical tape.

18. IT'S ALL ABOUT CONNECTIONS

We almost got bot! Now install the front whisker and make the final connections between power, the switch, and the control chip. There's no photo of these final steps, because they happen inside a semi-closed mouse. But you're such a circuit-hackin' fool by now that you don't need us anymore.

18a. Solder the black eyestalk wires to Pins 2 and 3 on the LM386.

18b. Solder the red battery wire to either of the side poles of the toggle switch.

18c. Solder a red wire from the toggle's center pole to Pin 6 of the IC, or to either Pin 1 or Pin 8 of the relay. Solder another red lead from the unconnected bump switch pin to one of these same locations.

18d. Cover all exposed leads and junctions with electrical tape to prevent shorts. Then glue or

Congratulations! It's a slightly anxious, light-seeking robot.

loosely tape your plastic "whisker" to the bumper switch, so that it clicks on impact.

18e. Finally, snap in the battery, and screw or tape the two mouse halves back together. Then put Mousey on the floor, switch it on, and watch it go.

FINISH

NOW GO USE IT »

USE IT.

ENJOY YOUR ROBOT MOUSE

MOUSEY GAMES

If all went well, Mousey the Junkbot's behavior will be apparent once you flip its tail. The robot should zoom away and eventually hone in on the brightest area in the room. It works best if you limit Mousey's surroundings to just one source of illumination – one light or sun-soaked window. Here are some other fun experiments:

Put Mousey in the hallway and close all doors except one. Make the open room as bright as possible, and see if Mousey eventually scuttles in there. Try orienting Mousey in different starting positions.

Tune Mousey's light sensitivity by bending the eyestalks. Move the stalks farther apart, closer together, and bent in different directions until you get the steering you're looking for.

Use a flashlight to lure Mousey around. This will drive pets insane! But be careful; agitated pets will attack your robot and try to rip its components out.

TROUBLESHOOTING A WAYWARD MOUSEY

If you turn on Mousey and nothing happens (cue laughing clarinet, "Wha-wha-WHAAAA"), or if it acts strangely, turn it off immediately. Something went wrong with the build. Here are a few things to check:

First, ask yourself the tech-support alpha question: is it plugged in? Make sure that the battery is new, the battery snap is well-seated, and its positive and negative wires are properly connected. Then make sure that bare wires, pins, and solder joints are not making unauthorized contact with one another. One sign that you may have such a short circuit is if the battery gets warm.

Next, double-check all solder connections against the instructions. Besides being in the right places, they should all be fat, shiny, healthy-looking joins. Use the multimeter to check resistances, and resolder anything suspicious.

If Mousey frantically spins in a tight circle, you've probably hooked the motors up incorrectly. Reverse the wires that connect to the motor on the side that's going backwards.

If it's a broader circle, the motors might be wired correctly, but just not level with each other. If so, reglue the motors so they're symmetrical and make sure the tires are the same size.

If Mousey's always heading backwards, swap the wiring on both motors.

RESOURCES

This project is adapted from my book *Absolute Beginner's Guide to Building Robots*. You can find schematics and installation instructions for additional Mousey hacks on my robot page at Street Tech, streettech.com/robotbook. More cool hardware hacks live in Dave Hrynkiw's *Junkbots, Bugbots & Bots on Wheels*.

To find other ideas for hacking your Mousey, and other LM386-based bots, Google "robot +LM386," "herbie +LM386," and "Randy Sargent +robot."

To learn more about DC motors, and see a dissected version of the motor used in this project, see http://xrl.us/fkxh.

RESURRECTING THIS OLD AMP

By Tom Anderson and Wendell Anderson

Vintage guitar amplifiers are available on eBay — brands like Fender, Vox, Marshall, Acoustic, and Sunn. We'll show you how to restore one of these old amps and make it sound as good or better than the day it was made. ⧉

Set up: p.113 **Make it:** p.114

TRANSISTOR AMPS DELIVER THAT OLD-SCHOOL SOUND

Musicians use vintage amplifiers for their uniquely satisfying tone. Old tube amps are expensive, but you can find solid-state models from the 1970s for less. Some audiophiles argue that transistor amps from this era have the best sound of all, because they don't burn out like tube amps and don't exhibit the crossover distortion found in many modern designs. We bought a few classic amplifiers on eBay, restored their vintage tone, and made them safer.

Tom Anderson and Wendell Anderson are engineers for an electronics company. As a hobby, they develop audio hardware and software projects.

KICK OUT THE OLD CAPACITORS BEFORE YOU KICK OUT THE JAMS

An electrolytic capacitor contains two intertwined rolls of aluminum foil. When the foil corrodes, the capacitor can no longer hold its charge.

Why Good Amps Go Bad

The main reason old amplifiers start to sound bad is because their electrolytic capacitors degrade. These fragile, liquid-filled components can corrode inside, leak, and even explode. Not surprisingly, such failures affect signal quality and can damage neighboring transistors and transformers.

— Foil
— Paper
— Electrolyte solution
— Insulating housing

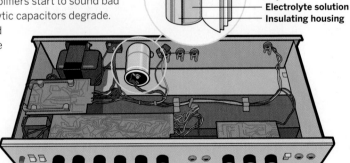

Illustration by Damien Scogin

SET UP.

Visit *makezine.com/02/oldamp* for source list.

WIRING DIAGRAM KEY

BFC = bulk filter capacitor
µF = microfarads (capacitance)
Ω = ohms (resistance)
FWBR = full wave bridge rectifier

L = line
N = neutral
G = ground
REV. RCV = reverb receive
REV. DRV = reverb drive

🔲 **Fuse**
• **Connection**
' **Diode**
⏚ **Ground** (from plug)
⎇ **Chassis ground**
⊣⊢ **Capacitor** (capacitance µF)
-W̌- **Resistor** (resistance Ω)

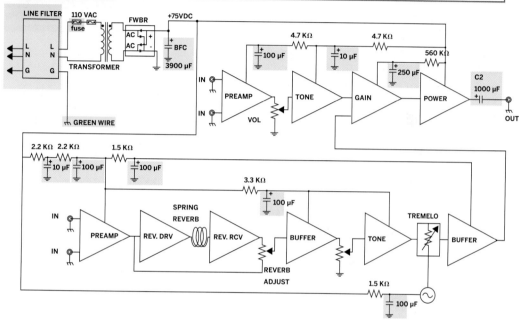

Before we get started, take a look at the circuit diagram above. It's a generalized schematic that should apply to most vintage transistor guitar amps. The parts shaded in blue are the ones that we are replacing. The main thing we're doing is swapping out the electrolytic capacitors, which will reduce hum and improve reliability.

We also added a modern line-filter module. This eliminates the need for a polarity switch, so you'll never suffer the old-rocker indignity of receiving an electric shock because the polarity's wrong. This is made worse with many old amps, where the power plug's ground prong has been hacked off. Installing a line module solves the power polarity problem once and for all.

Having the amplifier's schematic greatly simplifies the task of fixing it, because you can follow it along to find all the components you want to replace. We found many schematics in PDF format by searching Google for the specific model amplifier and "schematic." Others we bought online.

MATERIALS:

Vintage solid-state amplifier

Line module
Improve safety, convenience with a modular power cord

Heat-shrink tubing
Insulate soldered wire splices

Electrolytic capacitors
Replace old capacitors to reduce hum, increase reliability

Wire and connectors

Mounting hardware

TOOLS:

Digital multimeter
Read AC and DC voltages and currents

8Ω **Dummy load resistor**
Test amplifier at full power

Soldering iron, solder

Needlenose pliers

Wire strippers

File

Screwdrivers

Butane lighter
Apply heat to heat-shrink tubing

SCHEMATIC SOURCES:

schematicconnection.com/store/asp/default.asp

www.richbriere.com/The_Sunn_Shack.htm

univox.org

MAKE IT.

DIAGNOSE, OPEN, AND REPAIR YOUR OLD AMP

START ❯❯

Time: **An Afternoon** Complexity: **Low**

1. TRY IT OUT

Before opening the amplifier, you should inspect it for physical damage and wear. Then power it up and try the different controls. (Have a speaker and electric instrument on hand!)

DIAGNOSTICS	RECOMMENDATIONS
1. Look at the power cord and the entry where the power comes into the amplifier. Is the ground prong missing? Are the wires frayed or damaged?	1. Never plug a damaged power cord into an outlet! If the power cord is damaged in any way, the amplifier is unsafe. This must be fixed before any further diagnostics are attempted. Repair this before proceeding (see Step 5: Clean up Power Entry).
2. Plug in the amplifier, with speakers plugged into the output. Is smoke coming out of the amplifier? (Turn it off!) Is the amplifier humming or hissing with no input?	2. If the amp is smoking, unplug it right away. Keep a fire extinguisher handy. Hum can usually be fixed by replacing the capacitors, as described in this article. Hiss comes from the amp's first amplification stage, and is more difficult to fix because it usually requires some redesign of the amplifier. To learn about redesigning amplifiers, the best website is users.ece.gatech.edu/~mleach/lowtim/.
3. Plug in an input microphone or guitar. Is the amplifier alive? Is sound coming out that sounds like the input?	3. The sound test is the most important. If the amp is completely silent (absolutely no amplification under any condition), the power transformer may be dead. Power transformers are almost always custom-designed for the particular amplifier, and replacements are hard to come by. Consider using the amp as a gigantic paperweight.
4. Try out the knobs with the speakers plugged in. Are there scratches or intermittent signals when you turn the tone and volume knobs? Does wiggling the knobs up and down change the output?	4. If turning a knob causes clicks, pops, or dropouts, the knob's potentiometer needs to be replaced underneath. Pots are standard components. You might also try spraying a little contact cleaner into them. (Available at caig.com.)
5. Wiggle the input cord and the output speaker cord. Does this cause the signal to go intermittent?	5. If the cord connections are intermittent, replace the ¼" connector jacks. These are also standard parts.

WORKING IN ISOLATION

For safety, while testing your amp (or working on any other live, high-voltage circuits), plug into an isolation transformer. This reduces the possibility of electrocution. Even with the amp isolated, be careful not to touch across high voltage. You can avoid shocks by working with one hand in your back pocket. Also, don't lean on anything conductive, such as the amplifier chassis.

Photography and diagrams by Tom Anderson and Wendell Anderson

2. OPEN IT UP

2a. Many amplifiers are simply wooden boxes with metal boxes screwed inside them. The Acoustic 150 here only needed four screws taken off the top, and the metal box of guts slid right out. Make a diagram if you need help remembering where the parts go.

2b. Look inside the amplifier, checking for burn marks, loose wires, and structural damage. Burned up components usually indicate trouble. If they are resistors, use the multimeter to check that the resistor values are still correct. Broken hardware can usually be fixed or replaced. Rotted plastic can be replaced with hard metal. Pop rivets, PEMs, cable ties, or a squirt of Silicon RTV can replace many broken fasteners and mounts.

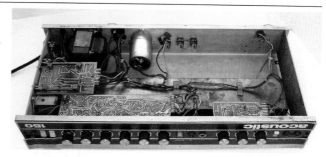

2c. Now we'll want to look at the power supply and measure the bulk filter capacitor (BFC) for replacement. Start at the power cord and trace it through the power switch to the large, heavy power transformer. At the output of the transformer is the bridge rectifier, a diode-based subcircuit that converts the ebb and flow of AC current into rough DC. This is fed to the BFC, which smooths the voltage out. Locate the BFC and note the maximum capacitance, working voltage, and surge voltage specs printed on the side. For capacitance, you can match your replacement BFC to the same value, or try one with a higher value to reduce hum. Don't go with too high a value, though, or you'll put too much stress on the full wave bridge rectifier. Next, we'll measure the voltage values needed for this cap in practice.

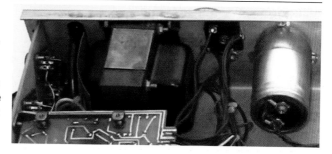

CAP CODE

This capacitor is rated at 3900 microfarads, with a maximum working voltage of 75 volts, and a maximum surge voltage of 95 volts. The capacitor's manufacturing "born on" date is decipherable from the last four digits of the cryptic number at the bottom, which probably denotes the year and week – in this case, the 17th week of 1973.

3. CHOOSE AND REPLACE YOUR BULK FILTER CAPACITOR

Capacitors fail when too much voltage is placed across them or when too much AC current is passed through them. So it's important to determine the maximum voltage and current requirements for the bulk filter capacitor, which handles the incoming power. This can only be done while the amplifier is operating at a full load turned up to eleven. Since this would ordinarily make a tremendous amount of noise, we fed the amp's output into an 8-ohm power resistor, to simulate a speaker with 8 Ohms of impedance.

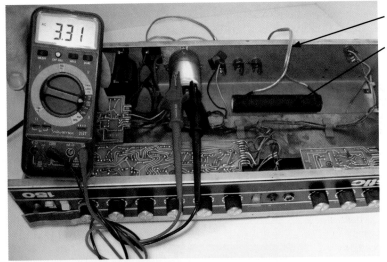

Speaker cable

8-ohm power resistor

WARNING: The load resistor gets very hot and smokes a bit! That's why we let it rest inside the metal chassis, so it wouldn't start a fire. We kept the fire extinguisher handy during this project!

3a. Disconnect the BFC's positive terminal, set the multimeter to measure AC current, and connect it as shown in the first diagram below, across the capacitor's two terminal connections. Use a clip and take care that the wire does not fall off, as this could blow the amplifier! At full power, our amplifier puts 3.31 amperes (A) of AC current through its BFC. Therefore our replacement BFC should probably have a ripple current spec of at least 3.5 amperes.

3b. Reconnect the capacitor, switch the meter to DC voltage, turn off the input signal, and measure across the capacitor. Ours read 74 volts (V). The voltage rating on the capacitor is 75 volts, so there is not much margin in this old amp.

3c. Armed with the values you need, buy a replacement BFC. The one we chose for our Acoustic 150 amp is the 4k microfarad (µF), 100V AA Series Panasonic Computer Grade Capacitor, which is rated at 100 VDC and 4.12 amperes of ripple current. We bought it online from Digi-Key, digikey.com. This capacitor has a 2" diameter, so it fits into the old capacitor's clamp.

Testing current/amperage

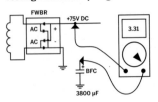

Testing voltage

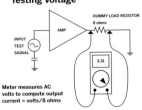

Meter measures AC volts to compute output current = volts/8 ohms

Calculating your amp's power output/wattage

Measure the voltage your amp puts across a dummy load, square it, then divide by the load. Our amp, cranked up, generated 33.4 volts across an 8-ohm resistor. This means that it has an output of 33.4 x 33.4 / 8 = 139.4 watts.

4. REPLACE THE OTHER CAPACITORS

The second most heavy-duty capacitor an amp needs is the output cap, which converts the all-positive signal into the plus-minus wave that speakers use. As with the BFC, the amp's other electrolytic capacitors can be replaced after measuring or calculating the voltages they need to be able to handle. Or you can just replace them to match what's already there and what you already know about the amp. You don't need to replace ceramic capacitors, because they don't wear out.

Like batteries, electrolytic capacitors have polarity. Look for little + or - symbols near one of the terminals. Don't get the terminals reversed, or the capacitor won't work. Worse, it can get very hot or even explode!

4a. For our output capacitor, we knew that our amp's maximum output voltage is about 33.4VAC. This makes the current through the capacitor 4.2 amperes, assuming an 8-ohm load, or a hefty 8.4A with a 4-ohm load. So we chose another 100-volt AA Series Panasonic capacitor, this one 10k µF, because it could handle about 10A of ripple current. The replacement was physically much larger than the original, so we bought a mounting bracket and found a spot inside the amp where the cap would fit, connecting it via wires, with heatshrink tubing over the solder splice.

4b. Unsolder and remove the capacitors on the printed circuit board. You can measure or calculate the voltage on each before choosing replacements, or make an informed generalization. Since this amp uses a 75-volt supply, we figured that 100V capacitors would work just fine.

Other than the BFC, the other capacitors in the amp have low ripple current. We used ordinary electrolytic capacitors with the same values, but with a 100V voltage rating.

CHOOSING ELECTROLYTIC CAPACITORS

Important electrolytic capacitor specifications include:
  A value or capacitance, in microfarads (µF)
  A working voltage, in volts (V)
  A maximum or peak voltage, in volts
  A maximum ripple current, in amperes (A)

Sometimes low frequency response can be extended and hum reduced by using a capacitor with a greater value, but it's safer to replace capacitors with the same value.
  For maximum reliability, a good rule of thumb is to use capacitors at 50% of their rated voltage. Don't exceed 75% of the maximum rated voltage.
  Ripple current specs are harder to find. They are not generally marked on the capacitor itself, but are buried in a table on the capacitor's datasheet.

5. CLEAN UP THE POWER ENTRY

The power supply starts at the power cord, then goes through the fuses, power switch, transformer, full wave bridge rectifier, and bulk filter capacitor. The original power supply used a polarity switch and several special capacitors across the AC line. A more modern way to do the same job is to use a filtered line module. A good module contains the equivalent of all these capacitors, and has another filter element called a common mode choke. Line modules are rated to carry a maximum current. Our Acoustic 150 takes about 2 amperes of line current, so we chose a line module rated for 4A. Line modules also use three-prong IEC connectors, which means the power cord can be removed and easily replaced if damaged.

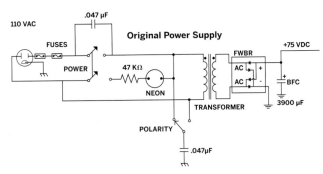

Original Power Supply

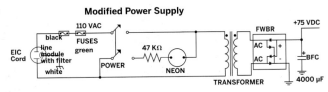

Modified Power Supply

5a. Unplug the amp and expose the power supply by unscrewing the side panel. On this amp, the panel hinges back with all the wires still attached.

5b. Make space for the line module to fit into. Our amp had an AC socket on the back to provide power to another piece of equipment. To create enough room for the module, we removed this extension outlet and filed the hole to widen it. Use duct tape and a piece of paper to keep the filings out of the amp — otherwise they might cause short circuits.

Line module

5c. Snap the line module into the chassis. The module's ground terminal will have a short green wire connected to a lug. Screw this lug into the chassis somewhere. This wire is the most important part of the amp, and must connect to the metal frame for safety.

Now close up the box. You're done!

FINISH

ENJOY YOUR NEW OLD AMP!

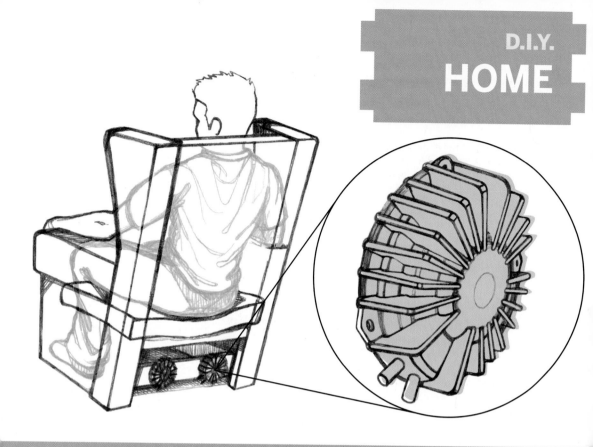

LET'S RUMBLE
Hack your couch to give you a kick in the pants.
By Craig Engler

Illustration by Damien Scogin

Bass shakers are like the rumble packs in a Playstation or Xbox game controller. They make whatever they're attached to rumble when they get a signal from the LFE (low frequency effects) channel of your audio system. That means when the T-Rex puts its foot down in *Jurassic Park*, you don't just hear it ... you feel it.

You can buy an $800 shaker system from a commercial outfit like Buttkicker or Clark, or you can put the components together yourself for as little as $30. I've done it both ways, and I like the $30 results better. That cost assumes you have some speaker wire and an old receiver or amp around. If you don't, plan on spending another $50-$100 for a used amp or receiver, plus $10 on speaker wire at RadioShack.

You can get the shakers at *partsexpress.com* or on eBay. When I bought mine, a pair of Aura Bass Shakers was going for $30, and the pro model was about twice that. People who've used both report little difference, so don't worry about buying the cheap pair. (I happen to have bought the pros before I found this out, so the ones shown here are the pros.)

For the receiver, make sure it puts out the necessary watts per channel (25 for the Aura, 50 for the pro) and you're set. Any speaker wire should do. You'll also need an RCA "Y" splitter and cable, which together run about $6.

Prepare to have many moving experiences with your bass shakers.

HOME

On my home theater chairs, I decided the best place to mount the shakers was on the back of the frame, underneath this flap.

Eyeballing it, I can tell the shaker will fit, but I'll only be able to fasten it with two screws. Ideally, you want to use four screws.

Use the RCA splitter on the subwoofer out line of your primary receiver. This way, you can send the signal both to your subwoofer and to the receiver you'll be using to power the shakers.

Once you've got your parts in hand, start by installing the shakers in your seating. One per chair is a good rule of thumb. If you have a couch, you may want more, but I'd start with one and see how much shaking you get. I didn't notice much difference in my three-seater couch whether I had one or four installed. I settled on two because a) I had extra shakers and b) I thought it might

even out the shaking effect more.

You can attach the shakers to any surface you can get four screws into, but you'll get the best shaking if you can fit them onto the longest part of your seating that's suspended between two points. On my couch, that was the piece of wood that ran the length of the seating, between the legs on either side. I had to pull off the underlining of the couch to do it, and then I used a staple gun to put the underlining back on after running my wiring.

If you're only using one shaker, make sure to center it, otherwise you might feel the shaking more on one side than the other (in other words, don't put them in the arms of your couch or chair). With multiple shakers, spread them out as evenly as possible. If you really can't find a place to screw them in, you can also use zip ties and attach them to the seating springs, but that won't transmit the shaking effect throughout the whole seat as efficiently. Still, in a pinch, it's a quick and easy solution.

Next, hook the shakers up. Start by splitting the RCA wire going to your subwoofer with the RCA "Y" splitter, and run the split signal into your

In the end, I mounted two shakers to each of my chairs. When I centered just one shaker on the frame, it hit the reclining mechanism of the chair when I leaned back. By using two equally spaced, I avoided hitting the reclining gear and also made sure both sides of the chair receive equal shaking.

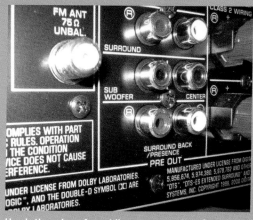

Here's the subwoofer out line on my receiver. Sometimes this output is called the "LFE out," which stands for "low frequency effects."

Photography by Craig Engler

amp/receiver with the RCA cable. Then, hook up the shakers to the amp/receiver's speaker outs with the speaker wire. The only trick here is whether to wire them in series or in parallel, which depends on how many shakers you're using. The instructions will tell you, or you can read the excellent "bass shaker" thread on the Home Theater Accessories forum at *avsforum.com*. I'd recommend reading that thread in any case, as it's full of good tips and information for trouble-shooting and modifications.

The rest you know how to do: Stick a DVD in your player, press play, and start watching a movie. When the explosions begin, your seat should respond with a perfectly synchronized rumble. You can control how much rumble you get with the volume control of your amp/receiver. I find the effect is best when it's subtle, so you can't quite tell if you're feeling your subwoofer or the shakers. But if you want your teeth to rattle, just pump up the volume.

To demo your shakers, I recommend the lobby and helicopter scenes from *The Matrix*, just about any scene from *Black Hawk Down*, the beach landing in *Saving Private Ryan*, the battle scene at the end of *Lord of the Rings: The Two Towers*, and my personal favorite, *Das Boot*. Also, make sure you don't tell your friends about your shakers before you invite them over. I find it's best to let them discover the shakers on their own.

Craig Engler's writing has appeared in publications ranging from *The New York Times* to *Wired*.

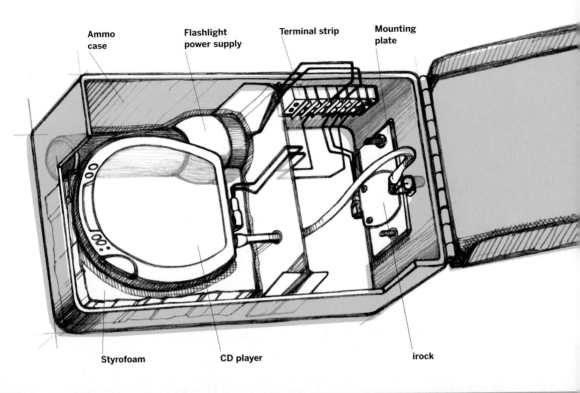

Ammo case — Flashlight power supply — Terminal strip — Mounting plate

Styrofoam — CD player — irock

IROCK BROADCAST BOOMBOX

Pump up the volume with a portable FM radio station. By Tom Anderson

Irock transmitters let you play audio from your iPod (or CD player) through your car stereo by "broadcasting" it via FM to the antenna just a few feet away. It's great when you're in a car, but what if you want to transmit over a larger area?

Using common electronics components and an old ammo box, I turned my irock into a portable microradio station with a range of about 200 feet. Instead of drawing power from a dashboard's 12VDC power jack, it uses a modified flashlight and two D-cell batteries, which run the rig for about 18-24 hours.

The main trick I found was to start by mounting the irock's printed circuit board onto a metal

plate, which I later secured inside the case at the end of the project. This way, I could do almost all of the delicate assembly out in the open. With all the drilling, it's also important to keep metal flakes off of the circuit board.

First, disassemble the irock by removing the three screws underneath the battery cover. Lift the board out, cut off the battery wires, and it's ready to mount. For the plate, I used a 3"x4" piece of 0.06-inch-thick aluminum, cut with tin snips, and then filed the edges smooth. Using the existing holes on the PC

An external antenna lets the irock realize its FM broadcasting potential.

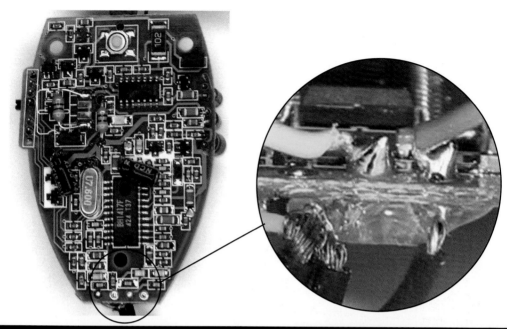

The antenna and ground connections for the irock's small, built-in antenna are located at the narrow end of its PC board. I'm simply connecting my own larger antenna to these two pads, by way of yellow and green jumpers wires and a coaxial connector. The irock's power supply also connects to this end of the board, so I soldered another wire pair to these connectors in order to bring the power outside of the ammo box.

board as a template, I drilled holes through the plate and bolted them together, separating the two with small plastic standoffs to avoid massive short-circuiting. Then I drilled a matching pair of holes in the ammo box. I also drilled two more matching pairs of holes through the mounting plate and ammo box.

Remove the board and plate, and drill another hole in the case, big enough for an F-type connector. This will be the jack for a 75-ohm coaxial cable that will carry the signal out to the station's external antenna. Locate the hole less than one inch from where the narrow front edge of the board will sit, right next to the irock's ground and antenna connections. Then solder a short pair of wires to the ground and antenna connections of the irock board.

Mount the irock board assembly back inside the box, and install an F-type connector in the hole, using a lock washer and a ground lug. My F connector from RadioShack did not come with a solder lug, so I took one from a BNC connector. Solder the wires from the board's ground connection to the ground lug and from the antenna connection to the F connector's center pin.

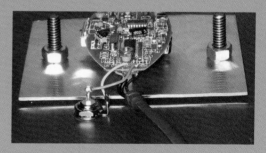

Circuit board on plate, with F connector and power line.

You can power the irock with any 3VDC power supply, but I used a rewired flashlight (see sidebar) and split the leads to supply juice to both the irock and the CD player, my audio source. To keep this conveniently switchable power supply outside the case during broadcast hours, I bolted a terminal strip to the side of the box. This became the power supply for both irock and player.

Inside, I soldered wire pairs from the back of the strip that were long enough to connect to the two devices, taking care to retain the correct polarity. I soldered the other ends to a 3VDC adapter plug and insulated it with heat-shrink tubing.

3VDC plug.

To prevent the box's guts from rattling around, the insides needed some structure. I used a metal divider, cut from an old piece of galvanized sheet metal. I shielded the sharp edges with duct tape, and duct-taped the partition to the inside of the box.

A styrofoam spacer underneath the CD player has a cutout for the flashlight, and the space can also hold CDs. The other side of the divider stows the antenna when the station is not in use.

To start broadcasting, connect a regular indoor FM antenna to a standard 75- to 300-ohm matching transformer (a.k.a. balun), and plug it into the box's antenna jack.

Matching transformer connected to FM antenna.

Hook up the player to the irock, and arrange them in the box so that you can still reach the irock's power and frequency selection switches. Finally, fire them up and see how far you're transmitting by moving around with a portable radio.

Wendell Anderson contributed to this article.
(Thanks to Bill Goldsmith of Radio Paradise for inspiring this article. Bill uses his modified irock to help monitor his 100% commercial-free station radioparadise.com.)

Tom Anderson and Wendell Anderson also wrote *Resurrecting This Old Amp*, page 110, in this issue.

Rewiring a Flashlight

A flashlight makes a good 3VDC power source, and it features a built-in on/off switch.

Remove the bulb, put it in a plastic bag, and use pliers to crush the glass.

Drill through the center of the bulb's base.

Thread some stranded wire through the hole; then strip the end, ball it up, and load it with melted solder. Solder another wire to the rim.

Pull the wire so the ball of solder presses against the bulb base, where it will contact the battery's positive terminal.

Now you have your two leads. Reassemble the flashlight, and test with a voltmeter.

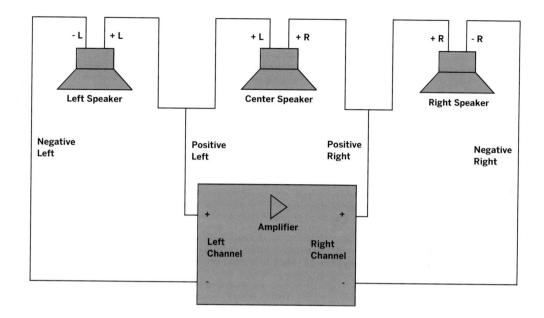

Left Speaker

Center Speaker

Right Speaker

- L   + L

+ L   + R

+ R   - R

Negative
Left

Positive
Left

Positive
Right

Negative
Right

+

+

Amplifier

Left
Channel

Right
Channel

-

-

SURROUND SOUND, QUICK N' DIRTY
A simple wiring trick derives center channels.
By Michael McDonald

Back in the late 1970s, I worked as a movie theater projectionist. That's when I learned this dead-simple trick for wiring a center-channel speaker to augment the right and left channels.

To do it, you wire the left and right speakers to the amplifier as usual, red to red and black to black. Then wire a middle speaker by connecting one pole to the amp's right red output and the other pole to the left red output.

This will take the signal that's shared by the left and right speakers, more or less, and put it in the middle. Then left and right speakers will produce only what is discretely left and right. Needless to say, the center speaker must be capable of reproducing a full range of sound. Add a fifth and sixth

speaker to a quad system, and you'll get true surround sound. The separation is great, even with low-dollar stereos (don't tell the Dolby and THX people). A good six-speaker arrangement would be to use two excellent speakers for front and rear channels with a four-channel stereo, and four less expensive speakers in the corners.

Audiophile purists may complain that adding speakers decreases the overall impedance and throws off the load balance between amp and speakers. But I've been using this hack in cars and homes for decades, always to great effect.

Michael McDonald is an inveterate geek who works for the federal government in Washington, D.C., as an IT specialist.

THERMOFOOLER

Who needs a "smart" thermostat when you can trick your dumb one into lowering your heating bill? By Ross Orr

Here in snow country, winter heating bills can get alarming (mine was $128 last December). Many people install programmable "smart" thermostats, which turn down the temp at night when you're in bed or during the day when you're away.

Good idea, but these $100-plus thermostats assume that each day, you robotically follow one rigid schedule for that day of the week. And you might have to program 28 different events and temperatures for your one-week cycle.

Forget all that. For about $3, buy an incandescent night-light — the kind that turns on and off with a photocell. Take a length of string and an extension cord, and hang this on the wall below your regular, "dumb" thermostat.

At bedtime, when you turn off the room lights, the night-light switches on and acts as a localized space heater — fooling the thermostat into thinking the room is warmer. You burn less fuel, and environmentalists cheer your virtuousness. Experiment with string length; the closer the light, the greater the effect. And unlike a "smart" thermostat, this adapts to your actual bedtime.

Morning light turns off the night-light and restores the normal thermostat setting. So if you get up before dawn, it could be a little chilly before you flip on the room lights. If you're feeling truly obsessive, you could plug the night-light into an appliance timer set to turn power off just before dawn, but that spoils the simplicity of things.

I'm still wondering how to adapt this idea for when the house is empty during the day. (Covering the windows would work for some homes, but my shades aren't opaque enough.) And what about my friends in Texas, where the scariest bill is for summer air conditioning? Any ideas?

Ross W. Orr hacks low-tech gadgets and invasive plants in Ann Arbor, Michigan.

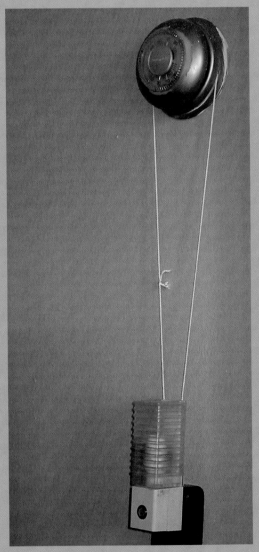

A light-activated night-light keeps your thermostat warmer at night.

Photograph by Ross Orr

Photograph by David Albertson

DVD, UNCRIPPLED

Input a special code to disable Macrovision and play DVDs from around the world.
By Phillip Torrone

About a year or so ago, I picked up a digital camera combo device — the Panasonic SV-AV30. This handy little $400 device records voice, video, and takes pictures. It's all low resolution, but fine for posting stuff to the web.

The AV30 includes a cradle that can play its recorded content to a TV/stereo (AV out) or record directly in (AV in).

A lot of devices that have "video in" — like the SV-AV30 and many of the new portable video players — can record from just about any video source, but if the signal is from something that utilizes the Macrovision video copy prevention technology, these portable video recorders simply will not allow recording of DVDs. It's kind of

ridiculous when you think about it. What good are these devices if you can't watch your purchased or rented DVDs on them?

The technology behind Macrovision is basically unwanted noise that scrambles or signals a chip inside a recording device to not record. When I try to record a DVD on my SV-AV30, I just get a warning screen.

Of course, there is a menagerie of applications that rip DVDs to allow you to copy the video to different kinds of players. But what I wanted was a DVD player that ignores Macrovision and would let me re-

Copy-protection: Just another mafia-style "protection scheme"?

127

Here's what happens when I try to record a DVD on my SV-AV30.

cord things just like I did in the good ol' VCR days. I wanted to pop in a DVD, press play, then press record on my devices.

With some research and eBay action, I scored one of the best DVD players that not only allows optional Macrovision playback, but can also ignore region encoding so you can play DVDs

from anywhere in the world. If you've ever bought a DVD while traveling, you've probably been let down by not being able to play it at home. What is this magical player I speak of?

The APEX AD-3201. I got mine for $50. On the outside, this is your run-of-the-mill DVD player; it plays DVD-Video, SVCD, CD, HDCD-encoded CD, MP3-CD, CD-R, and CD-RW, as you'd expect. It has the usual AV hookups, but this DVD harbors a gem of freedom. By inputting a special code, you can disable Macrovision and also play DVDs from any region.

Here's how:

1. Press Eject on the player.
2. Press 8 4 2 1 on the remote control.
3. There will be a new menu displayed, the Macrovision and Region code setup screen.
4. Press ENTER on the remote control to select the Region. Select 9 for Region Bypass (plays all DVDs).
5. Press the down arrow on the remote control to select Macrovision and press ENTER to turn Macrovision on or off.
6. To save the settings, press the eject button again to close the tray.

And that's all there is to it. Now, when I pop in a DVD I bought, I can record it to my SV-AV30. Here's the setup in action:

If you already have a DVD player, or don't care for the APEX player, there's a comprehensive list of DVD players, along with hacks to "free" them, at *videohelp.com/dvdhacks*. Happy hunting!

Phillip Torrone is associate editor of MAKE.

Photography by Phillip Torrone

SAVE ALMOST 42%

Make cool things

4 Quarterly Volumes of Make for only $34.95!

ADD THE **DIGITAL EDITION AT NO EXTRA COST!**

NAME (PLEASE PRINT)

ADDRESS   APT. #

CITY/STATE/ZIP

EMAIL

☐ Please add the companion Digital Edition at **NO EXTRA COST!***

*As the Digital Edition is only available to paid subscribers, we must have a valid email address to process your request.

MAKE will only use your email address to contact you regarding MAKE or other O'Reilly Media products and services that may be of interest. You may opt out at any time.

4 Volume Rate: $34.95. Savings based on $14.99 cover price. Canadian Rate: $39.95 USD (includes GST). All other countries: $49.95 USD. Sales tax as applicable.

For faster service, please order at **make.oreilly.com/offer**

Use your promotion code **B05BMB3**

O'REILLY

Make:
technology on your time

With iStopMotion software, creating stop motion animations could not get any easier.

STOP MOTION ANIMATION, THE EASY WAY

With iStopMotion, making *Gumby* is less pokey.
By Phillip Torrone

Stop motion animation, one of the oldest special effects, makes the impossible seem real. But the tedious process — move the model, take a picture, repeat thousands of times — discourages citizen filmmakers with non-obsessive patience levels.

I recently discovered iStopMotion, Mac software that automates the process and works with any camera that can capture QuickTime. iStopMotion features a transparent preview that lets you superimpose the previous frame over the current one before you shoot. This alone helps enormously. The Time Lapse feature shoots frames continuously at a specified interval, and Speech Recognition lets you say "Capture" instead of having to click. These two features saved

me thousands of trips back to the keyboard and mouse, and in just a few minutes of experimenting, I made a fairly impressive little flick.

You can even shoot frames simultaneously from multiple cameras, to create seamless cuts between different angles, just like the pros.

For inspiration, go watch *King Kong* and visit the example pages at *istopmotion.com/example*. I'll post my animation on the media feed of *makezine.com*. If you create one, let us know!

iStopMotion: free demo version, $39.95 license, *istopmotion.com*

Phillip Torrone is associate editor of MAKE.

Photography by Derrick Story

Capacitor

Discharge the flash capacitor before doing any work on circuitry!

SINGLE-USE DIGICAM FOR KITE AERIAL PHOTOGRAPHY

Simple, lightweight timer circuit triggers a shot every minute. By Limor Fried

Kite aerial photography (KAP) is a fun hobby for engineers and artists alike, and the resulting images can be beautiful. However, one unlucky gust can send your camera tumbling to the ground. That's why disposable cameras are a good choice for KAP beginners. Their low cost means there's no big loss if they crash. They're also lightweight, and most are pre-focused to infinity, which means they're good for taking scenery shots.

Many KAP rigs have been designed to take film-based disposable cameras aloft. (See MAKE Volume 01, for complete instructions on how to build your own kite aerial photography rig.) But film disposables require winding between shots, so you can only take one picture per launch.

Fortunately, there are digital equivalents that use electronic switches and need no winding. I use the Dakota Digital PV2; it's $19 at Ritz Camera (*ritzcamera.com*) and Wolf Camera (*wolfcamera.com*), with a $10, non-LCD version available in CVS stores. The PV2 holds 25 photos. As with a film disposable, you send it away for processing.

Here's how to make a kite-ready timer circuit that triggers the PV2 once per minute, after an initial delay. You can also adapt it to trigger other, non-disposable digicams.

Photography by Limor Fried

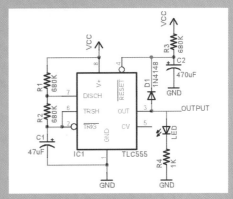

To run the Dakota PV2 from our timer circuit, we need to connect them with three wires: positive power (red wire, VCC in the schematic below), negative power/ground (black, GND in schematic), and the shutter trigger (yellow, OUTPUT in schematic). Conveniently, contacts for all three are arranged in a row on the PV2's top PC board, across from the shutter button. Our timer will piggyback off the camera's power source.

Designing the Circuit

Since it takes time to launch the kite, we'll want to delay the first shot. We'll implement this with a simple resistor-capacitor network. The capacitor slowly charges through a resistor until its voltage is high enough to turn on the timer chip, via the chip's reset pin.

The PV2 automatically shuts off after 3½ minutes idle, so our delay must be less than this. The time depends on the relative values for the resistor and capacitor, and I calculated that a 470µF capacitor and 680kOhm resistor (C2 and R3 in schematic at right) would produce about a 3-minute delay. (See *ladyada.net/make/sudc4kap* for full derivation.) Try this combination, and if the camera shuts off before having a chance to fire, reduce the resistor value.

For the main part of our circuit, we'll use a TLC555 or LMC555 timer chip. Configured with two resistors and a capacitor, 555 chips can generate square waves of almost any frequency up to 2MHz. We want to make ours oscillate every minute, firing a shot once per cycle.

Timing a 555 also uses an RC (resistor-capacitor) network. In our configuration, the 555 discharges a capacitor through one resistor and recharges it through two resistors in series. While the capacitor charges, voltage on the timer's output pin is high (3V) — and it's low (0V) while it discharges. I determined that a 47µF capacitor (C1 in schematic) and two 680kOhm resistors would tune the 555 to produce a 60-second square wave. (See website noted earlier for derivation.)

Other components in the circuit are an indicator LED that flashes once per cycle (for testing), and a diode between the Output and Reset lines. This keeps the Reset line voltage high, which protects against noise from the camera's flash that can trigger the shutter accidentally.

MATERIALS	Red LED
Single-use digital camera	Tape
Small perf board	
TLC555 or LMC555 timer chip	EQUIPMENT
470µF capacitor	Soldering equipment
47µF capacitor	Multimeter
680kOhm resistors (3)	Large flathead screwdriver
1kOhm resistor	Precision Phillips screwdriver
Switching diode (1N914 or 1N4148)	Needlenose pliers
Small toggle or slide switch	Angle cutters
Hook-up wire, preferably 22-gauge stranded	"Helping hands" or mini vise
	Solderless breadboard (recommended)

Fabrication

1. Disassemble the camera.

Take the batteries out, remove the three screws that hold the body together, and take off the back cover, being careful not to touch any of the electronics inside (they may be at high voltage).

2. Discharge the flash capacitor.

Carefully hold the main PC board as shown on page 130, making sure the vise or jaws don't short any exposed components. The huge capacitor carries the flash bulb charge, and it *must* be discharged before any hacking. Hold a flathead screwdriver by the plastic handle, and touch its tip to both capacitor leads simultaneously. There will be a large pop and flash as it discharges. (Do this again after any time the board has sat idle.)

3. Attach the control and power wires.

Cut three wires in red, black, and yellow (or other color) for the shutter wire. Solder these to the pins located where the top shutter board connects to the front flash board. Counting over from the shutter button, connect black to Pin 4, yellow/shutter to Pin 6, and red to Pin 8.

4. Reassemble the camera.

Thread the wires through the small hole in the flash board, and put the plastic case back on, so the wires come out the side. Then insert the two screws near the bottom of the case, and use a piece of tape to secure the top. Don't try to close the case all the way.

5. Build the controller circuit.

Before soldering your circuit onto the perf board, you should test it out on a solderless breadboard. Build the circuit following the schematic on page 131, making sure to place all the capacitors, diodes, and LEDs in the proper directions.

6. Test the circuit.

Connect the red and black wires from the camera to the VCC and GND points on the circuit, respectively. The LED should light up after two minutes or so, and then cycle on and off about every minute. Use a multimeter to confirm that there are 3V between the red and black wires, and check the voltage across the 470µF capacitor (C2) to make sure it rises slowly to 1V or so, then jumps up to 3V. Check the 47µF cap (C1) and look for slowly oscillating voltage between 1V and 2V. Finally, check the output voltage, which should flip between 0V and 2V, following the LED. If you're prototyping your circuit on a solderless breadboard and it all checks out, you should rebuild it, soldering onto the perf board, and test it again.

7. Test the full system.

With the camera off, discharge the two capacitors (C1 and C2) with the screwdriver. Connect the trigger wire to the OUTPUT line from the 555. Turn on the circuit, and then the camera. When the LED turns off for the first time, the camera should take a picture. (If it doesn't take a picture, try connecting the shutter wire to the black wire.)

8. Take flight!

Mount your camera and control board to your kite, and let it fly.

9. Disconnect the circuit and develop images.

After your flight, check the "Pictures remaining" counter to verify that the circuit worked. After all the pictures are taken, open the camera, discharge the flash capacitor, and desolder the wires. Then reassemble the camera and have it developed normally.

Limor Fried is a science genius girl (with apologies to Freezepop).

Forget jerky teleconferences; put a real lens on a '90s era webcam, and you've got something.

WEBCAM TELESCOPE
Video from still camera zoom. By Dennison Bertram

Photography by Dennison Bertram

If you're like me and collected all things new and digital during the '90s, then you have at least one old, ridiculously low-resolution webcam lying around. About a year ago, when I was living in a high-rise with great views across a large nature preserve, I figured out how to turn one of these things into a surprisingly good daytime telescope. By feeding the webcam's CCD with a telephoto lens from my 35mm camera, I got a video scope that could observe wildlife and identify license plates from quite a distance.

What You'll Need
Wood and screws: Any type of wood will do, but it must be thick enough to screw into the edges.

Flat black paint: For inside the box.

PC board standoffs: From any electronics shop.

Metal bayonet adaptor: These can be found fairly easily; try a camera repair shop. I got mine used for $15, and they cost about $30 new. Be sure to get one with screw mounts.

Webcam: Any webcam you can disassemble is fine. I used a Logitech QuickCam "eyeball" I had.

Lens: This hack works with any format and type of lens. I recommend a 35mm zoom telephoto. (You can even use a microscope, if you're interested in seeing really small rather than really far.)

Building It
First, measure out your wood for the box. The dimensions you want depend on two factors: it must be wide and high enough in front to mount the bayonet adapter, and deep enough to accommodate the focal length of the lens you're using.

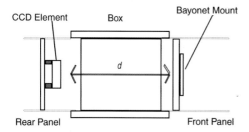

CCD Element   Box   Bayonet Mount

d

Rear Panel   Front Panel

The front of our wooden box has a mount for a camera lens, and the inside back panel holds the guts of an old webcam, with the CCD positioned at the lens' focal plane. Run the webcam software, then slide the back panel forward and backward in the box to put the CCD into proper position. With a telephoto lens, you get a daytime video telescope with a far better picture than you ever thought could come out of that webcam thing.

The webcam's CCD chip will be on the rear panel, so your box must be deep enough to put adequate distance between it and your lens. The unattached rear panel will slide backward and forward inside the box, allowing you to fine-tune the distance between bayonet and CCD for the best image quality distance (see diagram above). If you're working with a 35mm camera lens, then a box about three inches deep should be sufficient.

Cut the panels. On the box's front panel, sketch the place where the bayonet will be mounted, and then drill it out and mount the bayonet. Test your mount with a lens, to verify that the lens has enough space to slip in.

Then screw the box together, making sure the rear panel slides into the back. Add a small nick on one side of the rear panel, for the webcam's USB cable to exit out of. Then sink a couple of screws partway into the outside, to give you something to hold when you adjust the panel's position. Once you have your box mostly assembled, paint the inside flat black. This is called "flocking," and it minimizes internal reflections, increasing contrast and image quality.

Now disassemble your webcam, and take out the board with the CCD. (Don't you dare do this with your *real* digital camera.)

Center and mount the CCD onto the rear panel with screws and standoffs, making sure it's completely level. Attach your lens, and you're done!

Now that your box is finished, it's time to align the CCD with the lens. The best way to find the proper distance is to take your camera and measure the forward distance between its film-plane indicator (marked on top) and lens mount. This is the distance you'll want to replicate. Move the back panel to about the right depth for this.

Finally, aim the telescope at something far away, focus the lens to infinity, connect the webcam board to your computer, and jigger the panel back and forth until the image you're getting onscreen is sharp. To get the entire image field in focus, you'll also need to make sure that the CCD is parallel to the lens. This can be difficult when you're working with wood and screws. But try your best, and wiggle it around until you have image quality you feel satisfied with. Then have fun! Pretty cool, eh? Hey — no peeping into bedrooms!

DigitalniFoto Magazine columnist Dennison Bertram is an American photographer working in the Czech Republic.

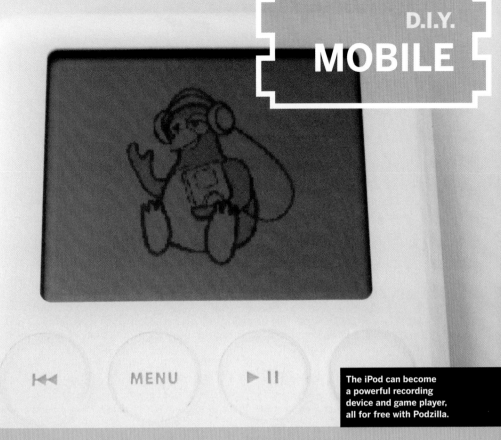

The iPod can become a powerful recording device and game player, all for free with Podzilla.

MOD YOUR POD

Enhance your iPod with a Linux upgrade.

By Phillip Torrone

Current estimates put the iPod population around 10 million. With that many brains banging on the same platform, a lot of weird mutations and modifications can crawl out of the muck, especially because the iPod is one of the more hackable players out there.

Here's a roundup of just some of the benefits when you Linuxify your Pod.

Changing the iPod's Operating System

Future civilizations will judge us by how many devices we had that ran Linux. Until recently, getting Linux on an iPod was fairly complicated and, at best, the resulting penguined iPod wasn't very useful. Things have changed. Installing Podzilla can give your iPod even more features (such as viewing black and white photos, recording high-

quality audio, and running new applications and games) while preserving the original iPod operating system.

Installing Linux (Podzilla) on Your iPod

At this time, Podzilla supports only first, second, and third generation iPods. That means the mini, iPod photo, Click Wheel 4G, and Shuffle are out of luck, but support for these models is expected to happen fairly soon.

Before you download the installer (*ipodlinux. org/installation*), it's a good idea to consider that what you're doing could damage your iPod. It's unlikely, but read the documentation and decide for yourself.

If you go ahead with the installation and something goes wrong or you'd like to roll back to regular ol' iPod, you can use Apple's restore utility (*apple.com/ipod/download/*) to return to the factory settings. It will, of course, erase all the data on the iPod.

Reboot to and from Podzilla on Your iPod

Once installed, you'll need to reboot. Press and hold Menu and Play at the same time for about three seconds. I installed mine so it would boot right into Podzilla, unless I press Menu + |<< (reverse) at the same time.

Now that we're kicking it Podzilla style, let's have some fun.

Podzilla Menu

When the iPod is booting into Podzilla mode, you'll see the familiar Linux boot screen whiz by and you'll be presented with a new iPod menu.

Most of the functions are self-explanatory: Music browses music, and Settings configures the backlight, contracts, wheel sensitivity, button debounce, and clicker. There is a Calendar and a Calculator as well.

Photos Without the iPod photo

With Podzilla, you can view 160x128 grayscale (four shades) photos in JPG, GIF, or BMP.

To make a photo you can view on your iPod, first create an image in your favorite image editing application and save it as a four-shade grayscale image. With the iPod in normal iPod OS mode, I made a folder call "pics" on the iPod drive. Then, reboot the iPod into Podzilla and use the File Browser to browse to the file and view.

Audio Recording with Podzilla

Apple limits recording with a microphone to 8kHz, 16-bit mono files, while the actual hardware is capable of a far higher sampling rate (up to 96kHz mono). Rumors abound as to why Apple does this, but no matter — Podzilla breaks the limitation.

Once you install Linux on your 3G iPod (audio recording works only with this model), you'll be able to record directly to the iPod using any microphone (or the included headphones).

Here's How: Press Menu to reach the main menu, and then press Extras. Select Recordings and scroll down to the Sample rate and choose 8, 32, 44.1, 88.2, or 96kHz. I generally choose 44.1kHz, as it seems to work the best in most recordings.

From here you can record using a microphone (I use a cheap powered one from RadioShack) or line in from another audio source. If you have the headphones plugged in, you can record by using the left earphone. Once you're finished recording, you can listen to the recordings (in WAV format) or boot back to the normal iPod operating system and grab them from the recordings folder. WAV files can be imported and converted in your favorite sound editing applications; I like to use the cross-platform and open source Audacity (*audacity.sourceforge.net*).

Bonus Tip: I recently picked up a Wireless Phone Recording Controller from RadioShack (Part # 17-855) for about $20, which allows you to route the audio from your cell or portable phone through a recorder. If you're into podcasting (see the *Podcasting* project, page 86) or just want to record conference calls and interviews to transcribe later, this is a good addition to your portable citizen journalist setup.

Games in Podzilla

Like games? Bored with the built-in Solitaire and Breakout? Tap Menu > Extras > Games and behold! A new catalog of cloned games: Asteroids, Othello, Tetris, Pong, and Minesweeper.

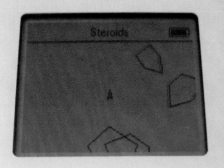

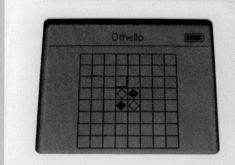

More?

There's a budding community of iPod Linux hackers. Be sure to check out the applications listing from time to time to see what's brewing. Some of the current projects in process include web servers and text editors (*ipodlinux.org/index. php/Downloads*).

Changing the Firmware

If you've ever restored your iPod to its factory settings, you've used Apple's restore utility. It's basically a copy of the firmware that resides on your iPod. This firmware contains all the graphics, text, and smarts that make an iPod work, but it's also quite modifiable using a free application called iPodWizard for Windows users. iPodWizard can modify all the graphics and text displayed on your iPod as well as add new display fonts. I

changed the annoying "Do Not Disconnect" flashing image, as well as the legal section of my iPod.

Here's How I Did It

Download and install iPodWizard, at *ipodwizard.net*.

It's a good idea to download the Essentials Pack, which includes the iPodWizard, along with tools to make it easier to modify text strings (the words you see on the iPod).

After you download and install iPodWizard, you'll need to find the iPod Updater firmware file on your system. If you don't have it, go to *apple.com/ipod/download/*.

Open iPodWizard and click Open Updater. The Updater is usually found in Program Files\iPod\ iPod Updater.

Click Open. Depending on what iPod you have, you'll need to select the firmware revision from the list.

Once you select the proper firmware, click Load. You now have access to all the changeable items for your iPod!

A quick tour of iPodWizard will reveal all the images in the user interface by clicking the |<< or >>| buttons, battery indicators, card faces for Solitaire, even the Apple logo. The buttons on the side allow you to load a new bitmap or save the current bitmap.

Changing a Graphic

To change the "Do Not Disconnect" graphic, choose the 89th image from the pull-down list. Save the bitmap by clicking Save Bitmap.

The image is a 100x100 pixel image that can be edited with any bitmap editor on your PC. I pasted in the MAKE logo and saved it. In iPodWizard, click Load Bitmap and import the bitmap you saved. From here you can click the Write button and you're finished.

For Mac users, two tools are available to edit graphics. By using alterPod (*podite.com/munity/*) and iPodIcons (*ipodicons.sourceforge.net*), you can extract, edit, and restore the iPod with the new iPod graphics you create.

Of course, you can do a lot more. (Give your daughter's iPod a Hello Kitty theme!) Check the iPodWizard forums (*ipodwizard.net*) to learn about mod ideas and to get new versions of iPodWizard Essentials.

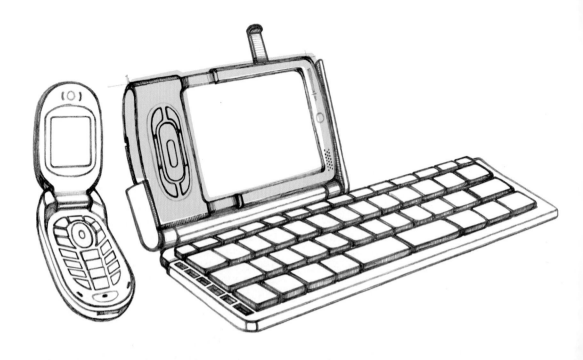

OUTFITTING A PALM TUNGSTEN T3
Getting laptop-like functionality from a PDA.
By Bob Scott

What's MAKE-able about yet another PDA? The Tungsten T3 is the first one I've found with the sophistication to serve as a viable, if limited, re-placement for a laptop computer at about a fifth the cost and a quarter the full-up weight. The key considerations are the generous screen, with a selectable portrait or landscape view, expandable memory, Bluetooth interface, and a wide array of peripheral components. Coupled with the arrival of viable office productivity software for the Palm OS, you can get a lot of work done with a minimal amount of carry-on luggage.

For writing, casual internet browsing, and email, I've found I can get by with three things: my T3,

a fold-up keyboard, and my Bluetooth-enabled cellphone. The setup is light, modular, and allows me to steal back otherwise wasted minutes of the day on the train, in lines, or at lunch. Given an unguarded flat surface, I can be typing on the T3 before I can even find the power cable for my laptop, much less waiting for XP to boot.

You'll need to plow through the offerings from Palm and their fleet of cottage industry suppliers to tailor a device to your situation, but I've found the following applica-tions to be a good start for most uses.

> **Leave your laptop at home: use a T3 PDA, loaded to the gills with powerful applications.**

Think Outside Stowaway Keyboard: Recently replaced by an IR interfaced version, I prefer this design for its passive (no battery) operation and rugged metal exterior. The dedicated hardware connection to the T3 is simple, reliable, and involves no fiddling with IR emitter sticks. Palm still offers a similar hardware interface keyboard that is worth checking out if you can't find one of these in stock somewhere. Make sure to download the latest drivers for whatever you get.

Bluetooth Phone with Data Access: Besides just being tidy, a Bluetooth link lets you grab information off the internet without even thinking about it. The PDA can silently link to a phone still on your belt or in your briefcase, allowing you to check your email or Google the status of your delayed flight while you're standing in a line (or bored in a meeting).

SD Memory Card: Bigger is better, so get one at least twice the size of the internal memory of your device. That will let you do a backup and still have some storage space for other items.

Documents to Go: This hefty software package is well worth the memory it will chew up, allowing you to create, read, and update Microsoft Office documents, spreadsheets, and presentations on your handheld. Supporting both portrait and landscape views, it makes the most of the screen space on the T3.

WEBPRO Browser: Included with the T3, this also supports landscape display and can handle most websites, as long as they don't need exotic features (e.g., ActiveX components). I've used it for everything from restaurant recommendations to paying bills on my bank's website.

Snapper Email Client: Not cheap, but it goes well beyond a basic POP3 client, easily handling IMAP servers, SSL links, attachments, and much more.

Backup Software: It's rare, but the Palm OS occasionally melts down, particularly if you like using a lot of third-party software.

Having a handy backup copy of all your data and software can be a lifesaver on a trip. I'm using Botzam Backup, which executes automatically

every day. I don't have to think about it until I need it.

Mission Specific: Too numerous to list, but this includes anything peculiar to your profession or hobbies. Everything from serial terminal emulators to planetary motion predictors are available. Also think about special purpose hardware like Wi-Fi SD cards, modems, printers, VGA outputs, etc.

The T3 was recently replaced as the flagship Palm OS platform by the Tungsten T5, resulting in some terrific price cuts. I got a refurbished T3, a one gigabyte SD memory card, and a hard case for well under what the T3 was retailing for just six months ago.

(A refurbished Tungsten T3 goes for about $250, and a one gigabyte SD card can be bought for as little as $75.)

Bob Scott is a statistical construct of various consumer-electronics marketing departments.

Save your Spot
Let your camera phone serve as a backup for your brain. By Phillip Torrone

Pain is a wonderful motivator. The time I couldn't remember where I parked my car during a Minnesota winter inspired me to figure out a system so it never happens again. By now, most us have phones with cameras. We use them for a couple of weeks and then forget about them. The killer app for these phones is a quick photo of where you parked. Each time I park at a mall, airport, or anywhere there's more than a floor or acre of cars, I take a photo. It's never let me down — it's saved me hours of trying to remember, "Was it the blue asparagus floor, or the pink fourth floor?"

Bonus Parking Hack: If your phone has a voice recorder (many do), you can use that instead to tell yourself where you parked.

Illustration by Damien Scogin

Orb streams your stored content from your PC to your handheld devices.

ALL-SEEING ORB

Your mobile device can play video and music stored on your home computer. By Phillip Torrone

When I first heard about Orb Networks and its bold promise to give me free access to my home computer's stored music, photos, videos, and live TV from any phone, Mac, or PC, I almost dismissed it as an empty promise from a company touting vaporware. But I was surprised — it just works, which is about the best thing anyone can say about a technology that promises so much.

The install took under a minute. Once installed on your Windows machine, Orb asks you which TV system you use. The TV program guide data is processed, and within a few hours you're able to access live and recorded programs. You use your login and password to access content from any web-enabled device. I tried plugging my USB web camera into my home PC. My devices could then display whatever my camera was pointing at.

Orb does all the heavy lifting. It keeps track of the IP addresses as they change. It transcodes the content so it is specifically optimized for the device you're viewing it on. Photos are the appropriate size for the screen you're viewing. When I used my phone to listen to podcasts, the interface looked great.

Unfortunately, you can't play DVDs in the ROM drive or iTunes music, but anything Windows Media can play seems to be the domain of Orb. While Orb will work on just about any XP machine with a TV tuner, including the Media Center PC, there isn't any Mac support. If you travel a lot, store most or all of your media on a PC at home and have high-speed access in hotels, airports, and such; then Orb is a dream come true.

Download Orb for free at *www.orb.com*.

Photograph by Phillip Torrone

An out-of-the-box Maxtor drive. Note the absence of a power switch. Bad Maxtor, bad!

PEACE AND QUIET WITH THE FLIP OF A SWITCH

Adding a power switch to an external drive.

By Joe Grand

To me, there is nothing more annoying than the din of a spinning hard drive and a whirring fan, 24 hours a day, 7 days a week. I bought my 80GB Maxtor Personal Storage 1394 drive with a plan for it to act as an offline file server and backup depository.

To my surprise, there was no power switch on the unit. Maybe it's just me, but it seems that any product that isn't required to be on all the time should provide some method for the user to turn it on and off. Maxtor's design decision didn't make sense to me, so it was time to take matters into my own hands.

Since I only use the drive periodically, it doesn't need to be on all the time. The hack

was conceived and completed in 30 minutes and finally gives me peace and quiet when I'm not using the drive.

This hack demonstrates some key basic elements of hardware hacking and serves an immediate, practical purpose. Add an easily accessible power switch to the front of the external drive to enable and disable the drive without having to struggle with disconnecting the main power supply and risk dropping the power supply cable behind your desk.

Tools and Materials

The only components we'll need for this hack

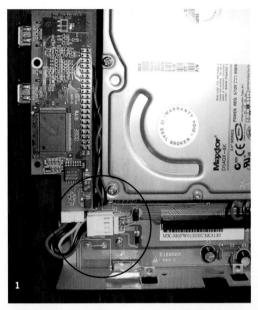

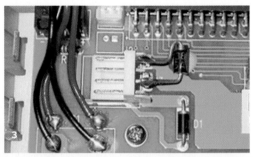

WIRING THE SWITCH

1. Unplug the daughterboard from the main circuit board.

2. Clip the two connections on the board where a switch was meant to be mounted.

3. Add wires to the four pads of the switch connection.

are four lengths of 20- or 22-gauge wire and a DPST (double pole, single throw) rocker, toggle, or slide switch. You could use a DPDT (double pole, double throw) switch if you happen to have one of those lying around instead (you just won't use all of the connections on the switch).

You'll also want to have handy a Phillips screwdriver, wire clippers, soldering iron and solder, and a Dremel tool, drill, or hobby knife.

As always, be sure to take proper safety and anti-static precautions, as the drive's control circuitry is sensitive to static electricity and you wouldn't want to damage anything.

Take the Drive Apart

Begin the hack by removing the plastic side rails that hold the two main pieces of the drive's housing together. These rails are attached to the drive with plastic clips and come off relatively easily.

With the side rails removed, you can open up the drive by pulling apart the two halves of the plastic housing. The main circuitry where the power connector is located is underneath the metal shielding. Remove the two screws that

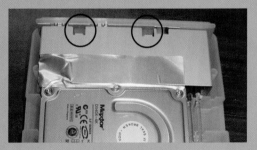

Remove the two screws from the metal shielding.

hold the top of the shielding in place.

The control circuitry for this Maxtor drive is made up of a main circuit board, containing most of the power connections, and a daughterboard, containing the interface circuitry. Remove the daughterboard by gently pulling it straight up and off of the main circuit board. You can leave the two wire harnesses connected to the daughterboard and just set the whole board aside.

Looking closely at the main circuit board, it becomes immediately obvious that the Maxtor drive was designed to contain a power switch, but wasn't included in the final production unit!

Photography by Joe Grand

Clip, Cut, and Solder

In place of the power switch are two wires shorted between the connections, essentially simulating a switch permanently in the "on" position. This makes our hack especially easy, as the connections we need are made available for us in those four easy-to-access locations. Clip the two wires on the board, leaving just the solder connections.

Next, strip and tin the four lengths of wire. These will be used to connect the switch to the pads on the circuit board. The length of the wire will vary depending on where you decide to mount the switch, but around 15 inches each should be good. It is helpful to use two red and two black pieces of wire in order to keep track of the connections on the circuit board. Solder the two red wires to the top two pads on the circuit board and solder the two black wires to the bottom two pads.

Now, modify the top housing to fit your particular switch. Prepare to get covered in plastic filings as you drill, Dremel, or cut your way into the case. Once you've hacked your case to fit the switch, put the switch into place and solder the four wires to it. With the switch held horizontally, the two red wires should be soldered to the top two leads of the switch and the two black wires should be soldered to the bottom two leads of the switch.

When the switch is in the "on" position, the two red wires should short together and the two black wires should short together. When the switch is in the "off" position, none of the wires should be connected to each other. Double check your connections and verify the functionality of the switch before applying power to the drive, because if the wires are not soldered to the right locations on the switch, you could damage the drive's power supply circuitry (and possibly much more). A red wire should never come in electrical contact with a black wire.

Finishing Up

At this point, the actual "hacking" part of the hack is complete and you should have something similar to the following photo. Remember to reattach the daughterboard to the main circuit board before testing your creation.

Front plastic housing with a switch successfully added.

Once you're sure that your new power switch actually turns the drive on and off, you can screw the metal shield back into place, close up

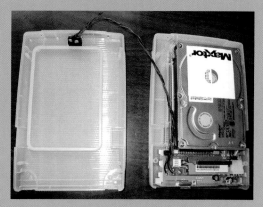

Successful hack ready to be buttoned up.

the housing, and reattach the plastic side rails. Make sure that the sides of the housing aren't pinching the wires. And there you have it: some peace and quiet with the flip of a switch.

Peace and quiet with the flip of a switch: the modified Maxtor drive (front view).

Joe Grand (joe@grandideastudio.com) is the president and principal electrical engineer of Grand Idea Studio, Inc.

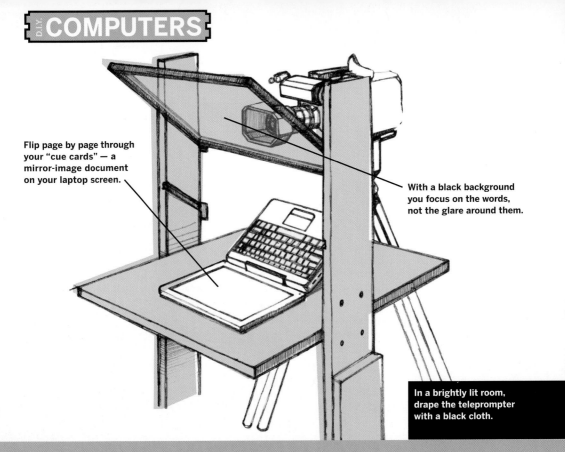

Flip page by page through your "cue cards" — a mirror-image document on your laptop screen.

With a black background you focus on the words, not the glare around them.

In a brightly lit room, drape the teleprompter with a black cloth.

NO MORE CUE CARDS

Make a teleprompter with a laptop, a sheet of glass, and some scrap wood. By Brian P. Lawler

It was Thursday evening, and I needed a teleprompter.

I was making a video about panoramic photography, and in the scenes where I spoke directly into the camera, I looked like a cross-eyed newscaster. While trying to read cue cards on a stand in front of the camera, my eyes were cast downward, and that looked odd.

To overcome this problem, I decided to build a teleprompter. Having seen commercial tele-prompters over the years in television studios and at trade shows, I understood the concept.

A teleprompter is made of a sheet of glass suspended in front of the camera lens at a 45-degree angle. The glass reflects the image of a TV screen without affecting the light entering the lens.

My prompter is nothing more than a sheet of window glass supported in a plywood frame in front of the camera at the correct angle. I probably spent three hours cutting and building.

Once it was done, I set my PowerBook on it and put a mouse with an extension cord on my knee to click when I wanted to change pages. White letters on a black background worked best, and I had to output the pages as mirror images using a page layout application.

With my home-built teleprompter, the recording of the narration went smoothly.

Brian Lawler is a college teacher, photographer, graphic artist, woodworker, and writer who lives in San Luis Obispo.

Excerpted from *creativepro.com*. Copyright ©2005.

Illustration by Damien Scogin

Two thankful robots
pose for their creator.

ROBOT KITS AND TECHNO GLITZ

Three kits that got me started in the glamorous and fulfilling world of robotics. By Arwen O'Reilly

Growing up, I read more Jane Austen than science fiction, and spent hours dreaming of the elegant past. But now, with more and more articles detailing the leaps and bounds in robotics (some good, some bad), I've started to prick up my ears. If our world will soon contain robot nurses for the elderly and robot tanks with remote-control guns, I need to start learning more about robotics.

A robot kit seemed the best way to start, so I checked out three: the Parallax Boe-Bot, the Lego Mindstorms Robotics Invention System 2.0, and a kit based on the book *123 Robotics Experiments for the Evil Genius*. Each has its strong points; the choice is really about how you like to learn. I also

heard about two kits in development: the PICO Cricket and the Vex Robotics Design System.

Parallax Boe-Bot: Manual Labor

Parallax's Boe-Bot is the classic workhorse of the bunch, powered by two wheels with separate servo motors, and programmable in BASIC. Once assembled, it looks like a small tank, with with its squat metal chassis supporting the printed circuit board. Boe-Bot's thick instruction manual slowly takes you through simple mechanics and the basics of, well, BASIC – spending a sadistically long time on preliminaries before having you actually start building.

But once you do get the hang of things, there is something magical about commanding those whirring servos by typing on the screen, and it makes the actions of your little creature very real. The Boe-Bot is a great way to learn both robot-building and programming, and the experience will teach you to appreciate roboticist Rodney Brooks' words from *Fast, Cheap, and Out of Control*: "Don't try to control the robot, but feel how the world is going to control the robot."

Lego Mindstorms: Candy-Colored Robots

Lego Mindstorms tries to make every step as colorful and exciting as possible; they even apologize for the plain box that the kit is shipped in. Inside, it's the treasure chest you dreamt of as a child, each compartment filled with a high-saturation puddle of Legos. Vivid diagrams show you various bot incarnations you can snap together, and I assembled six before bothering with any programming (sometimes I like my dessert first). Then I listened to the instructional software's excessively cheery narrator explain how to script in RCX, which isn't any more interesting than learning BASIC, but is a lot prettier.

In RCX, you literally drag language components together to build series of instructions. Representing common code elements as icons like this makes the process quick and intuitive. This great if you only want an IF > THEN > GOTO understanding of robotics, but you won't be learning a real programming language.

The Mindstorms website hosts a great forum where you can share ideas with other Lego roboticists, so once you've built all the suggested structures, there's a whole other world to explore.

Bots From the Bottom Up

If you want to build your robot from scratch, family-run Hobby Engineering sells all the components used in Myke Predko's *123 Robotics Experiments for the Evil Genius*. This book (which already comes with its own printed circuit board) is completely charming. Predko starts out with robot structures and basic electrical theory, then gets into the more serious stuff: opto- and audio-electronics, digital logic, sequential logic, sensors, and finally, programming. Like the Boe-Bot (and other Parallax offerings), Predko's design centers around a BASIC Stamp 2 microcontroller.

The book is nominally for kids, but there's no sacrifice of intelligence or quality of information. Building Predko's robot is far more time-consuming than starting with the Parallax kit, and you'll have to solder and cut plywood. But the end product is completely yours. If you truly want to learn how to build a robot, this is the way.

Beyond Basic Bots

By the time this article goes to press, RadioShack will have released its Vex Robotics Design System, a programmable robot kit with over 500 parts, including a six-channel radio controller, three variable-speed motors, multiple gears and wheel types, and a configurable chassis. It looks like an Erector set on steroids. And Playful Invention Company is introducing its PICO Cricket kit, which builds interactive sculptures, musical jewelry, and other things that control light, color, music, and sound. It's more of a multimedia kit than a strict robotics offering, but it might bring a new audience into the fold.

And that fold is one of the nicest parts of learning about robots: roboticists are enthusiastic and eager to help. If we're destined to share more of our lives with robots, that's a very good thing.

Visit *makezine.com/02/robotics* for source list.

(Thanks to Dave Mathews, Al Margolis, Julie Stern, Mitchel Resnick, and the boys at Squid Labs.)

Arwen O'Reilly is MAKE's editorial assistant.

Photograph by Saul Griffith

The Seiko 7S26 can be
modded with a variety
of aftermarket dials and
other components.

MECHANICAL WRISTWATCH MODDING
Customizing a self-winding Seiko. By Bob Scott

Photography by Bob Scott

Who still owns a mechanical watch? Well, me for
one. It's the original micro-technology.

I got hooked on "high-mech" several years
ago, as I became fascinated with the intricacy
and cleverness of design involved in getting a
mechanical device to precisely and repeatedly
"tick" despite variations in temperature, gravity
(i.e. position), and maintenance.

Mechanical watches seem almost alive
compared to their digital counterparts, offering
aesthetic interest and longevity in place of the
extreme accuracy and cheaper-to-buy-new-than-
repair approach of their quartz cousins.

Mechanical watches are also accessible to the
amateur. A small set of tools and some practice

are all that you need to master basic watchmaking skills. A practical use of these skills is customizing the look of a watch to your exact requirements or style preferences, which brings us to
the family of watches based on the Seiko 7S26
movement.

This rugged, fairly accurate mechanical movement features a self-wind mechanism, day, date,
and the usual hour, minute, and second hands.

Aesthetically, the kindest thing that can be
said of it is "unremarkable." A product of machine
finishing and largely robotic assembly, it's not
going to make any watch enthusiast light-headed
when opening the back. But that also engenders
one of its greatest strengths: it's cheap! New

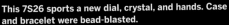

This 7S26 sports a new dial, crystal, and hands. Case and bracelet were bead-blasted.

7S26-based watches start as low as $50 on eBay, with the high-end retail for some fancier models only around $300.

Used in everything from the small "SNX427" military series of watches to massive mechanical diver's watches, the 7S26 has been in production for years and has spawned a modest number of after-market dials and other bits.

Shown in the photo is a modified 7S26-powered Seiko diver's watch. I picked up the base watch for under $100 on the used market. The dial and hands were purchased from a company in Pennsylvania and are based on a Vietnam-era military design. The stock mineral glass crystal was replaced with an anti-glare sapphire version, which is almost impossible to scratch.

The case and bracelet were bead-blasted to remove the stock shiny chrome plating. The bead-blast process leaves a utilitarian matte finish to the underlying stainless steel and is often mistaken for titanium.

If you'd rather build a watch up from scratch, there are several firms that can supply you with cases, bare movements, hands, and dials. Usually designed for repair work, these parts are relative-

ly easy to bring together in a unique, inexpensive "Frankenwatch" with a little practice.

The easiest way to get started in amateur watchmaking is to take an online course or study with an instructor, if you're lucky enough to have a training facility nearby. Then, pick up a few cheap mechanical watches at garage sales or flea markets to practice on. Don't expect to repair your first finds; just learning to disassemble and reassemble them is rewarding enough initially and will teach you what you need to know to parts-swap properly fitted hands and dials.

References
Timezone — discussion, used watches, and courses
timezone.com

Mark II Watches — custom parts and watches
mkiiwatches.com

International Watch Works — repairs and service
internationalwatchworks.com

Poor Man's Watch Forum — great for project ideas
pmwf.com

Bob Scott is a statistical construct of various consumer-electronics marketing departments.

Photography by Mark R. Brown

Within this joystick lies the heart and soul of a favorite old Commodore (no, not Lionel Ritchie).

HACKING THE C64 DTV

Retro-gaming joystick easily converts into full Commodore computer emulator. By Mark R. Brown

Retro gaming is the latest craze, and Mammoth Toys is letting people rediscover 20-year-old videogames by making a joystick that mimics 30 classic Commodore 64 games, including Paradroid, Uridium, Impossible Mission, and World Championship Karate. It plugs right into your television — no console required. QVC sells the C64 DTV (Direct-to-Television) joystick for $30. At a buck a game, it's a real bargain.

The ASIC chip at the heart of the C64 DTV simulates the original C64 while doubling the RAM and offering 16 times the color palette. (That's, um, 128K and 256 colors.) But there's far more to the DTV, thanks to a development team that clearly was not satisfied with just software bonuses. They loaded the DTV with undocumented hooks and features, and, not surprisingly, the toy has a cult following of Commodore-happy joystick modders.

Without even cracking the case you can boot the joystick up in C64 mode, run "secret" games, find numerous Easter eggs, and summon an onscreen keyboard that lets you write and run BASIC programs from the C64 command line.

And if you pull the DTV apart and look inside, you'll see that the circuit board is littered with helpful labels and unused, hack-inviting solder pads. On the C64 DTV hacking forums that have sprung up online, people exchange notes on all sorts of modifications, from enhancing the audio to kludging up a flash memory module. In short, the C64 DTV is a hacker's dream: a Commodore 64 for the 21st century. Is it any wonder that the C64 community is excited about this thing?

Hacking the Hardware

The DTV hacking community has come up with some pretty fancy modifications for the joystick platform. We're going to turn ours into a full-fledged Commodore C64 clone by adding a power supply, a disk drive, and a keyboard (not that we don't enjoy entering text with the joystick). If you can handle a screwdriver and a soldering iron, doing this is easy, and, after cloning the C64, you can jump off into your own custom hacks.

Parts List

A "wall wart" power transformer that puts out 5-volt DC or less, at 800 milliamps or better. You've probably got at least one of these in your junk pile. But before you go soldering, test it with a multimeter to make sure it's not putting out more than 5V. I've found the DTV to be pretty robust, but you don't want to fry its power regulator.

A PS/2 keyboard. You can use an older one with a large connector, or a new one with a small connector. Just stay away from really old XT-style keyboards. They won't work.

A Commodore 1541, 1571, or 1581 disk drive with at least one compatible floppy disk. If you don't have a drive in the attic, you can pick one up on eBay. Check that it comes with a cable. If not, you can look for a super-cheap, used Commodore drive cable (see links at end of article), or buy a new one for about $10.

TOOLS:

Medium Phillips and small flat-head screwdrivers
Soldering iron (less than 30 watts, with a fine tip) and solder

Hobby knife
Multimeter
Solid hookup wire (24-gauge)
Shrink-wrap tubing or electrical tape
Frosty beverage

Build the Clone

Start by taking out the DTV's batteries. Then unscrew four Phillips screws on the underside of the joystick's base, and separate the base from the top with a small flat-blade screwdriver, being careful not to pull any wires that connect the two.

Cut the plug off your power supply, plug it in, and use a multimeter to identify the positive and ground/negative wires. Then unplug it. Inside the DTV, use the knife to scrape the silicone off the battery contact terminals on the underside of the top half. Solder your transformer's positive wire to the terminal that connects to the red wire, and the ground wire to the terminal with the black wire. Plug in the supply again, and make sure the DTV's power LED lights up when you turn it on.

Power supply done; now, the keyboard. Cut your keyboard's connector off, strip some casing off the plug side, and use your multimeter to associate which color wires run to each of the different pin positions in the keyboard's plug. There are two sizes of PS/2 plugs, with different pinouts. Write down the correspondence between the colored wires in the cable and their functions, as listed below for your connector.

Big XT/AT Connector (plug side)

Pin	Function
1	Clock
2	Data
3	Not connected
4	Ground (power -)
5	+5VDC (power +)

Small PS/2 Connector (plug side)

Pin	Function
1	Data
2	Not connected
3	Ground (power -)
4	+5VDC (power +)
5	Clock
6	Not connected

Now it's time to remove the DTV's two circuit boards. Four Phillips screws hold the main board, and two more secure the smaller joystick button board. Remove them all, and lift out the board assembly, being careful not to let the seven red plastic joystick buttons fall onto the floor and roll under your workbench.

Flip the board assembly over and find the four rubber pads that serve as joystick contacts. Pop off the rubber pads located at 12 and 3 o'clock when the joystick board is facing up.

Find the five solder pads marked by the three arrows in the photo to the right; they're clearly marked KEYBOARDDATA, KEYBOARDCLOCK, IECCLK, IECDATA, and IECTAN. These are where you'll be connecting the keyboard and disk drive.

Prepare four 3" to 4" pieces of hookup wire. Then strip some casing from the keyboard cable,

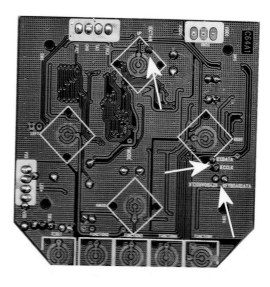

On the underside of the DTV's top half, we'll connect our power supply and the main board's keyboard power terminals to the battery contact terminals shown above.

The DTV's main PC board has clearly-labeled contact points for attaching a peripheral keyboard and disk drive, indicated above. Talk about hacker-friendly!

spread the wires, and refer to your color-function correspondence to find the Data, Clock, +5VDC, and Ground wires. Fire up the soldering iron and use the hookup wire to connect the first two to the KEYBOARDDATA and KEYBOARDCLOCK pads, respectively, and the +5VDC and Ground wires to the terminals that you already soldered your power supply to.

You can insert and solder the wires from either side of the board, but it will be easier to reassemble things if you insert them from the component side. Use heat-shrink tubing or electrical tape to wrap the joints. (Wiring the keyboard directly to the power terminals like this, bypassing the switch, means that it draws power whenever the DTV is plugged in — and that's OK.)

Plug in the power supply, turn on the DTV, and hold down the keyboard's K key as it powers up. The DTV should boot directly into BASIC mode. If you get the normal game menu, check your connections and try again. Some people report having to reboot several times before the DTV recognizes the attached keyboard. Then power down and unplug before continuing.

Now let's hook up the disk drive. As with the keyboard, you'll splice the cable and probe the wires to identify their different functions by their plug pin positions, using the chart below. We'll only use four: Ground, Attention, Clock, and Data.

Disk Drive Serial Connector (plug side)

Pin	Function
1	Service Request (SRQ)
2	Ground
3	Attention (ATN)
4	Clock
5	Data
6	Reset

You can probably guess what's next. Solder three more lengths of hook-up wire to the pads marked IECCLK, IECDATA, and IECTAN (which is a typo for IECATN), then connect the other ends to your drive cable's Clock, Data, and Attention wires. Finally, solder the Ground wire to the power supply ground terminal.

Now you just need to reassemble everything. Feed the tips of the connector pad plugs through the holes on the board, then pull them gently through from the other side. Replace all the red buttons, put the board in place, and secure it back with the screws. Drill, carve, or use a Dremel tool to cut a hole in the DTV's base that's big enough to feed the cables through.

Plug the other end of the drive cable into your Commodore drive and turn it on. Fire everything up, holding down the keyboard K to boot into C64 mode. Insert your floppy and enter LOAD "$",8. You should hear the drive spin, and the DTV should load the directory from the disk. Enter LIST to see the disk's contents.

Cable-tie the internal wires together, to provide enough strain relief that you don't accidentally pull them out of the board. Carefully route the wires out the hole, snap the base back on, then reinsert and tighten the four case screws.

You are now the proud owner of a brand-new, improved, 20-year-old computer. Ain't it cool?

Now What?

If you just want to download and run C64 programs, pick up an XE1541 cable, which hooks a Commodore drive to your PC so you can transfer downloaded disk images and programs to C64 floppies. Find out more at *sta.c64.org/xe1541.html*.

If you're an assembly language programmer, check out the free Turbo Macro Pro+DTV assembler at *style64.org*, which gives you access to the DTV's expanded color palette and extra memory. You might also want to hack an S-video output to replace the sometimes-funky DTV composite video and separate the mono audio output into three discrete synthesizer voices. Or you might hack in a second joystick. For these and more ideas, check out the sites listed below.

C64 DTV Links

C64 DTV Yahoo! group
games.groups.yahoo.com/group/DTVTalk

DTV hacking site and forum
www.orrville.net/dtvhacking

Project 64 — C64 doc archive
project64.c64.org

Funet C64 software archives (US mirror)
ibiblio.org/pub/micro/commodore

Mark R. Brown was Managing Editor of <i>.info</i>, the legendary Commodore computer magazine.

Secret Software Tricks

When you turn on the C64 DTV, you briefly see the famous Commodore "Chicken Head" logo and a credits screen. Then the C64's standard blue prompt screen appears, and the lines LOAD "*",1 and RUN are entered, as if by a ghostly typist. The screen clears after this, and you're presented with the regular game menu.

Interrupting the blue screen during startup will fork you over to lots of hidden extras. Hold down the left joystick button during startup, and you'll get to the regular games menu faster. Quickly wiggle the joystick left and right during startup, and you'll get to the C64 Mode menu, which offers six bonus games and "Basic Prompt."

Select Basic Prompt (the left joystick button selects), and you're in BASIC mode, a clone of the C64 blue screen and prompt, with the command-line interface. From here, you can summon a joystick-controlled onscreen keyboard by holding down the left joystick button. To type, navigate around the keyboard, then release the left joystick to enter the character you're on. Repeat as necessary. The SH (Shift) keys act like Shift Lock, remaining on (or off) until toggled back again. (The Commodore 64 keyboard is quite different from a PC keyboard. If you're unfamiliar with how it works, visit the online manual at *lemon64.com/manual*, and refer to section 2.1, Communicating with your 64: The Keyboard.)

From BASIC mode, you can list the programs in ROM by typing:
```
LOAD "$"
LIST
```
To run the "Entropy/Electron" demo, a favorite interactive art piece from the early "Demo Scene" era, go to BASIC mode and type:
```
0 POKE1,55:LOAD"ENTROPY",1
RUN
```
Then go through the screens by holding down the A button while pushing the joystick up for a few seconds each.

The C64 DTV also has numerous Easter eggs. Here are two, and others are documented at *xrl.us/fmzm*. To see Commodore legend Jim Butterfield drinking beer with a friend, type:
```
LOAD"1337",1,1
RUN
```
Finally, speaking of elite, you can bring up a picture of some members of the C64 DTV development team from BASIC mode by typing:
```
LOAD"DTVTEAM",1,1
RUN
```
The full team includes Jeri Ellsworth (manager), Jason Compton, Adrian Gonzalez, Robin Harbron, Per Olofsson, and Mark Seelye.

GAME BOY HACKS

Games, music, movies, photos, and eBooks, all on this versatile little device. By Phillip Torrone

The old-school Game Boy Advance is great for plane rides and DMV queues. But hauling a billion cartridges around wastes precious man-bag space — and I tend to lose them. I looked for a way to put all my games on one cartridge, and found a cool solution that also lets me play music, view photos and movies, and even run UNIX.

The key to it all is a piece of hardware called the Flash Linker & Card Set (*gameboy-advance.net/ flash_card/gba_X-ROM.htm*). It costs $89 but it's worth it. Compatible with the Game Boy Advance and GBA SP, it's based on a special cartridge that fits into your Game Boy, holds 512MB of flash memory, and connects to your PC via USB. The flash cartridge can carry up to 32 of your cartridge games, and lets you access thousands more as downloadable freeware. With free emulators, you can translate and play games from other systems, and the cartridge can also hold videos, music, eBooks, and photo albums.

Getting Started

Before you plug anything in, download and install the software that controls the communication between the Game Boy and the PC. You'll need the X-ROM driver and LittleWriter, both available at the website listed above.

Use the cable to connect your Game Boy to your PC. (The instructions say you shouldn't plug into a USB hub, but it worked for me.) Then, power up the Game Boy and hold down both Start and Select. The LittleWriter app on the PC should detect the Game Boy, and once it loads, you can back up your game cartridges to the PC, or transfer new games stored on the PC over to the flash cartridges. The games are all stored and accessed as GBA (a.k.a. ROM) files. It took me about an hour to back up all of my game cartridges.

Free Game Boy Games

A Google search of "Gameboy Advance ROMs" [sic] will yield thousands of games. I like a lot of the freeware homebrew titles on *gameboy-advance-roms.tk* and *pdroms.de*.

To copy GBAs into the flash cartridge, drag them into LittleWriter's ROM window, and click Flash. Booting up with this cartridge will then offer a menu with all the games. Freeware games are typically smaller than licensed cartridge titles, so you can fit more of them into flash.

Game Emulators

You can play games written for other platforms by translating them from their original formats into compatible .GBA ROM files, using an emulator. I've tried free GBA emulators for games from Sega Master System (SMS), Nintendo Entertainment System (NES), Super Nintendo Entertainment System (SNES), the original Game Boy, and even the old Sinclair ZX computer from 1982. (I'm especially fond of Super Metroid, from the SNES.) You can find emulators for these and other machines linked from *gameboy-advance. net/gba_roms/emulated_on_gba.htm*.

...And Other Delights

The emulator principle extends to other media besides games, and free converters have sprung up that let you convert a variety of files types into .GBA files, including video clips, music, slideshows, and text-file eBooks. The site above links to these as well. For music, you first need to convert the file(s) to .PCM format in your favorite sound editor. The sample rates can be 16,000, 11,025, or 8,000 Hz — 11,025 worked fine for me. Stereo doubles the file size, so use mono for spoken word.

Meanwhile, there's even a UNIX project for the Game Boy Advance. I didn't have the proper files to compile the ROM to get this to run, but here's a guide: *kernelthread.com/publications/gbaunix*.

Phillip Torrone is associate editor of MAKE.

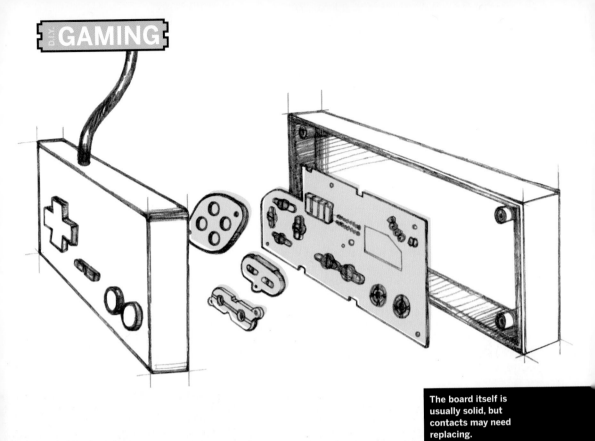

The board itself is usually solid, but contacts may need replacing.

REFRESHING AN OLD GAME CONTROLLER

If your retro-gaming skills ain't what they used to be, fix your joystick buttons. By Ben Wheeler

If you play vintage game systems, you'll sometimes find that Mario won't jump on command, or Ms. Pac-Man pauses when moving left. No wonder: the Nintendo Entertainment System (NES) controller just celebrated its 20th birthday, and Atari, Intellivision, and Commodore 64 controllers are even older. Over the course of the hundreds of sessions in a controller's life, metallic connectors beneath the buttons and direction pad can wear away and no longer complete the circuit that registers a keypress event. Luckily, it's a simple matter to refurbish old controllers and make them responsive again.

Unrefurbished NES controllers are available on eBay for about $5, and may come in any condition. Controllers for older systems can run $5-$20. Refurbished, guaranteed controllers can be quite a bit more: seller-certified Atari 5200 controllers, the most expensive, go for $30.

Vintage controllers fall into two categories: analog joysticks (Atari, ColecoVision) and digital direction pads (NES, Super Nintendo, Intellivision, Sega Master System and Genesis, PlayStation original). Joysticks have more complicated, if elegant, internal mechanisms. Direction pads are easier to fix because they are just a set of buttons overlaid with a piece of plastic. (Modern analog controllers used with PlayStation 2, GameCube,

Illustration by Damien Scogin, photography by Ben Wheeler

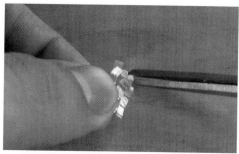

When you press a button, conductive material on its underside bridges two adjacent contact terminals on the circuit board, registering the keypress event. Not surprisingly, decades of vigorous play can wear the buttons out. But aluminum foil brings that old feeling back. After sticking a bit of foil under each button with double-sided tape, they'll once again make immediate, voltage-conducting contact with the terminals underneath.

and Xbox, like old analog controllers, can't be repaired as easily.)

On the earliest controllers, for the Atari 2600 and 5200, Intellivision, and ColecoVision, the internal circuit is printed on flimsy plastic, rather than fiberglass. If these circuits are worn out, you'll need to buy a replacement circuit (around $6 on eBay) as well as replace the contacts.

MATERIALS:

Aluminum foil	Double-sided tape
Scissors	Screwdriver

1. Unplug the controller from your console. WARNING: Always unplug a controller before opening it, and don't plug it back in until it is screwed shut.

2. Unscrew and open it. The screws may be small, so don't strip them with a screwdriver that's too large. When the controller is open, find where the buttons contact the circuit board. Most controllers use rubber to make the button resist. Wipe the metallic contacts on the underside of the rubber with a dry cloth or napkin.

3. Make the replacement contacts. Cut little squares of aluminum foil, one for each button. They should be about ⅛" wide. Affix them in rows to a piece of double-sided tape.

4. Replace the contacts. For each button, cut off a square of foil, with tape attached, and stick the tape side to the metallic contact. Press firmly so that the foil flattens evenly and sticks well.

5. Close it back up. Replace all parts as you found them; if your controller has an analog joystick, you'll have to align the joystick's vertical and horizontal teeth with their proper sockets. Then close the controller and screw the cover back on.

6. Test it. Plug the controller back into your console, fire it up, and enjoy a new level of vintage sensitivity! If any buttons are overly sensitive, the foil underneath may be off-center or not flat.

Ben Wheeler is a math teacher living in Brooklyn, N.Y.

With a $20 app and some light hackery, a PSP will play anything.

GET AN iLIFE! FOR YOUR PLAYSTATION PORTABLE

Play music and vids on a PSP (even Mac users).
By Phillip Torrone

With the release of Sony's PlayStation Portable (PSP) comes the usual disappointment at Sony's lack of out-of-the-box support for the Mac. While the PSP does have a USB mode that allows universal access to its Memory Stick Duo, and the Mac crowd can use a Duo stick to shuttle data (more on that later), this is where the crumbs of kindness end. Fortunately, a ravenous developer community has released some amazingly intuitive applications for Mac and PSP. With free and shareware applications, along with some information on how the PSP stores its data, you can sync music, photos, and video from a variety of sources when you plug your PSP into your Mac.

PSP Data Storage

The PSP primarily uses Sony's proprietary Universal Media Disc (UMD) format for games, video, and large media files. While it is rumored that Sony may open up the UMD format for anyone to read and write with, I'm not holding my breath; I lived through Betamax, Minidisc, and ATRAC. UMD packs 1.8GB of data into its 60mm diameter optical disc. This usually consists of games, music, and movies. But I'm not looking forward to paying over and over again for the content I already own on other media.

Anyway, the PSP offers another way of accessing its data, by using the Memory Stick Duo card.

Photography by Phillip Torrone

The Memory Stick Duo comes in 64MB to 1GB flavors; you can usually score a 1GB for under $150. A 128MB Memory Stick Duo stores roughly 100 2-megapixel images, 60 minutes of 280kbps/QVGA video, or 130 minutes of 132Kbps encoded music. Read/write speeds hover between 20Mbps to 160Mbps, depending on the hardware, with Sony stuff talking to Sony stuff.

I have a Sony digital camera, and so I have amassed a small collection of Memory Stick Duo and Duo Pros. Unfortunately, when you format or use the Memory Stick Duo in the PSP, not all the required folders are present by default for viewing all types of data, such as video. But if you get into the stick's file system, create a new folder, name it to follow the PSP's own internal naming conventions, and fill it with videos (properly encoded), you can play videos on the PSP. That's what we're going to do.

Formatting the Memory Stick

The best way to start is to format the Memory Stick on the PSP. To do this, pop the Memory Stick in, power up the PSP, and in the main menu, scroll all the way over to System Setting. Press O, scroll down to Format Memory Stick, choose Yes, and press O again.

From here, there are two ways of viewing the folders that the Memory Stick created. You can pop the stick out and use some type of flash card adapter. (I have a 6-in-1 that I picked up for $10; just make sure it handles Memory Stick Pro — some don't.) Alternately, you can go into USB mode on the PSP and access the file system from your computer via a USB A to USB 5-pin mini cable. These cables are handy for synching, so if your PSP didn't come with one (mine didn't), you might want to make the investment.

To use USB mode, plug the USB cable into your Mac, then plug the mini USB connector into the PSP. Power up, and on the main menu, scroll all the way to the left and select Setting; then scroll down and choose USB Connection and press O. On your Mac you'll now see a new Untitled disk. That's your PSP; let's see what's on it.

Memory Stick Files and Folders

At the root level, there is a MEMSTICK.IND file. This keeps track of the content on the Memory Stick, and is of no specific interest to us now.

Double click the PSP folder; inside are four folders: GAME, MUSIC, PHOTO, and SAVEDATA. What is stored in these folders is pretty obvious. GAME is for downloaded games, and SAVEDATA is where the Sony UMD games store their scores and game states. (I haven't tried it, but I assume you can trade saved data from games with pals to get ahead in levels.)

MUSIC holds MP3s and M4As, and in fact, you can drop some in there right away and play them. The downside with Sony's bare-bones MP3 implementation is that it doesn't read ID3 tags or album art, and you can have only one level of subfolders under the MUSIC folder.

Also, keep in mind that DRM-protected content, like the content from the iTunes Music Store, will not normally play (you can remove the DRM, but that's another article; check *makezine.com* for more). Later, I'll show how to automatically sync this folder up with iTunes. For now, just drop MP3 files in here and they should play just fine.

Next up is the PHOTOS folder. I dropped a few dozen JPEGs in here and they played well. I'll show you in a bit how to sync automatically with iPhoto.

Video Folder?

Where is the video folder? There isn't one, at least not at this time. My guess is that Sony wants to either sell you a tool to make videos, which will then automagically appear on your Memory Stick ready to play, or they hope you'll pick up a UMD video disc. Luckily, Sony has used the same folder hierarchy on devices for years, and it's easy to add the two new folders you need.

Back out to the root level of Memory Stick. You should see the folder PSP. Create a new folder called MP_ROOT, open that folder, and create a new folder inside that called 100MNV01.

If you had properly encoded and named videos, you could drop these in now, but it's likely you won't until you convert some. We'll do that later, after we sync up some music and photos using the iLife applications.

iPSP

One of the first and best applications to use on a Mac with the PSP is iPSP (*kaisakura.com/iPSP/index.html*). The application costs $20, but you can download a free, limited-capacity demo to see if you like it. You could, of course, transfer all the

There are two ways to get into your PSP: the Memory Stick port and the 5-pin mini USB port. To transfer data from a computer to your PSP, you can write it onto the Memory Stick with a card reader, then swap the card into the PSP. With MacOS-based machines, a slicker solution is to connect your PSP directly to your computer with a USB A to mini-USB cable, then use iPSP software to transfer the files.

content manually, but to perform big synch jobs effortlessly, iPSP is worth the shareware fee. The main features of iPSP are:

Games: Automatic game save and backup
Music: iTunes Playlist integration (supports Smart Playlists)
Photos: iPhoto Album integration (supports Smart Albums)
Video: Multiformat queue-based video converter with multiprocessor support
Synching: Automatic

iPSP Video Encoding

iPSP's game, iTunes, and iPhoto interfaces are easy to pick up. But the video encoding deserves some further explanation. Theoretically, iPSP should convert almost any video you throw at it, but some files won't work or will lose their audio track. My best advice is to experiment. MPEG generally works as an intermediate format, smoothly converting to and from anything else. But it's not an exact science.

Looking for videos? A great source for free video content is *www.archive.org*. I download many classic films as well as the latest Red vs. Blue cartoons here. And, depending on where you live, your local laws, and your relationship to those laws, you may be able to convert DVDs that you own and DRM-protected TV you record into PSP-friendly formats such as MP4. Check out upcoming articles on *makezine.com* for the latest information on what's possible.

iPSP's video encoder has a fairly straightforward video settings panel, with a slider for Animation to Live Action, the size of your Memory Stick, Quality settings, and bitrates. iPSP can handle all this automatically, but for better control of how you ration your video quality over your Memory Stick space, you can choose your own bitrates, as explained in the sidebar on the next page.

The highest quality video setting on the PSP is 1,500Kbps, and I've found anything over about 400 plays fine for my viewing.

Sadly, you cannot make videos larger than 320x240 (QVGA). The native resolution for the PSP is 480x272, which seems to be reserved for UMD videos and gaming. Luckily, the few pixels do not matter much when watching videos made in full-screen mode.

By default, video converted with iPSP saves to the folder /Users/you/Movies/iPSP (you can change this in Preferences), and has a filename between M4V00001.MP4 and M4V09999.MP4. iPSP also creates a thumbnail file, but this need not be transferred to the PSP.

Encoding Video Without iPSP

If you don't want to shell out the $20 for iPSP, and you're happy manually transferring files, you can convert videos with the free tool altShiiva (*hetima.com/psp/altshiiva.php*). The instructions are in Japanese, but the menus and text are in English, and the application is easy to figure out. altShiiva lets you crop and scale, and even optimize, for the PSP. The resulting file can then be transferred to the PSP through USB, or directly to the Memory Stick via a reader.

Watching Video on the PSP

To play your video on the PSP, pop the Memory Stick in and/or disconnect USB Mode. Scroll all the way down to Video-Memory Stick on the main menu, and press O; your videos will appear here. Press O to start or △ to get info, delete, or play. While the video is playing, adjust the size by pressing △, and select the screen icon adjust aspect ratio (4:3 or 16:9). If you created good-quality video, zooming in to fill the screen will result in a pretty amazing, smooth-playing video.

More Hot PSP-on-Mac Action?

To me the PSP and Mac are complementary. I use my Mac to store and create lots of videos, music, and photos, and the PSP is great for carrying all the podcasts, photos of my dog, and TV/DVD/videos that I bring and make on the road. And the PSP plays games, too! I look forward to many more applications and hacks for the PSP in the coming months, especially from Mac folks like myself who like to mash these things together. We'll keep you posted on *makezine.com*.

Calculating Maximum Bitrate

When you're choosing a video bitrate to match your available space, remember that the file size comes from video plus audio. If L represents the length of your clip, then the size of the clip's video component is L times your video bitrate, while the audio component takes up L times your audio bitrate. In other words:

$S = (L \times ARate) + (L \times VRate)$
Where:
S = Total size of clip (usually in MB or KB)
L = Length of clip (in minutes and/or seconds)
$ARate$ = Audio bitrate (usually in Kbps)
$VRate$ = Video bitrate (usually in Kbps)

Since your audio bitrate will probably have a standard setting that you already know, you can solve this expression for video bitrate and then plug values in to determine your target. The expression above, solved for video bitrate, is:

$VRate = (S / L) - ARate$

Let's say you want to fit a 30-minute video into 250MB (the usable space of a 256MB Memory Stick), while retaining the original audio bitrate, which is a standard 15.5Kbps. Remembering that 1MB = 1024KB, 8 bits = 1 byte, and 1 minute = 60 seconds, you get:

L = 30min x 60sec = 1,800 seconds
S = 250MB x 1024KB = 256,000KB
$Arate$ = 15.5Kbps / 8 bits = 1.9KBps

Plugging these into the expresson above:

Vrate = (256,000KBps / 1,800s) - 1.9KBps
 = 140.32KBps x 8bits/byte = 1,122.58Kbps

Therefore, you won't be able to go over a video bitrate of 1,120Kbps and still fit your video on the Memory Stick.

R2-DIY

THE GALAXY'S MOST LOVABLE ROBOT INSPIRES ITS FANS TO CLONE HIM.

By Howard Wen

"I found R2-D2 to be the funniest Star Wars character. Since I saw the first movie, I envisioned having one of my own," recalls Federico Sesler, a 30-year-old economics student in Rome, Italy. "I wanted an R2-D2 that could run around the house and attract people's attention with its amusing sounds."

So he made one — his very own full-scale R2-D2. And he's not alone.

Over the last five years, building replica R2-D2s has grown into a serious hobby scene. The R2 Builders Group, one such internet community dedicated to this craft, counts more than 2,400 members. R2 builders take great pride — perhaps obsessively and a bit protectively — in the detail they put into their reproductions of the familiar Star Wars android.

There tends to be a uniform size and look to these fan-made R2s, making them virtual copies of the real thing. That's because many makers use a particular set of blueprints based on the actual R2-D2 prop used in the movies.

A build-your-own R2 is made with any number and combination of materials. Wood is commonly used for the interior framework; plastic, fiberglass, resin and machined aluminum usually comprise the exterior. Some builders even make R2s with metal components, inside and out, for sturdier results.

Those people new to the craft of building an R2 are advised to start by constructing what is basically a display model, and then later add working lights and the ability for it to emit the familiar beep-boop sounds of the character. Next in skill difficulty is installing radio-control drive mechanics, so that the R2 can be driven about on wheeled legs and its dome head rotated by remote control.

Speaking of the legs, the most mechanically complex — and show-stopping — thing to build into an R2 is the ability for it to extend out, and set into

> "We had to redesign the middle leg deployment and retraction. The original R2 unit would only drop the leg, not raise it. So we actually went further with it than the original designers did."

position, a third leg from underneath its barrel-shaped housing, and retract it. Among R2 builders, such a feature is referred to as a "2-3-2" (an R2 that can change itself from "2-leg mode" to "3-leg" and back). The R2-D2 prop in the first Star Wars movie couldn't even pull this off.

"As a group we had to redesign the middle leg deployment and retraction. The original R2 unit would only drop the leg, not raise it. So we actually went further with it than the original designers did," says

Photography by Dan Goldberg

R2-DIY

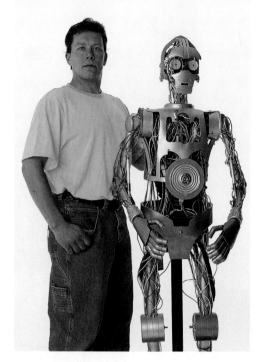

Kelly Krider, a 30-year-old sign maker from northern Illinois, who successfully 2-3-2ed his own R2.

Not content with constructing big remote-control toys, the R2 builder community is in the early stages of implementing artificial intelligence (AI) technologies, using lightweight PC components like notebook computers, to turn a homemade R2 into a real robot. Research into this so far has consisted mainly of using infrared sensors so the R2 unit can avoid obstacles in its path and vocal synthesizers so it can "speak" to people who walk by it.

It may be a while before a hobby-built R2 can autonomously perform even the simple actions of its movie counterpart. When a 15-inch-tall interactive R2-D2 toy was released, some R2 builders hacked them to use their electronic brains to drive their full-size R2s. "My 15-inch interactive R2 is quite uncontrollable and catches furniture without realizing it," says R2 builder Craig Smith, a 36-year-old spa-and-pool service technician from Milwaukee, Wisc. "I shudder to think of a 135-pound R2 running into things and still going!"

A malfunctioning R2 is not an option for many of these builders. Besides showing off their R2 at Star Wars and science-fiction/fantasy conventions, a number of them use theirs to cheer up kids in

Left: Kelly Krider's R4-N4 astromech robot has two 24V scooter motors in the feet for remote-control driving. Right: Craig Smith (described by a fellow maker as a "one man Droid Factory") with a C-3PO-inspired android.

children's hospitals or rent them out to businesses promoting the release of a Star Wars-related product.

Therefore, an R2 has to be on its best, non-injurious behavior. R2-D2 is a cute robot, not a killer cyborg, after all. So, in the same way that the R2 prop is operated behind-the-scenes in the movies, a fan-made R2 unit still needs the human touch to give it the unique and lovable personality of R2-D2.

"I feel AI is not at the point yet that I can trust to put it in a 100-pound robot," says Alexander Kung, a 39-year-old applications engineer from Toronto. "I once had a young girl run up to my R2 and give it a hug that lasted five minutes. I don't know if AI would be intelligent enough to know not to move."

The R2 Builders Club
www.robotbuilders.net/r2/

Astromech.net: Droid Building Resource
www.astromech.net

Howard Wen is a freelance writer who has written for *oreillynet. com, salon.com, playboy.com,* and *Wired,* among others.

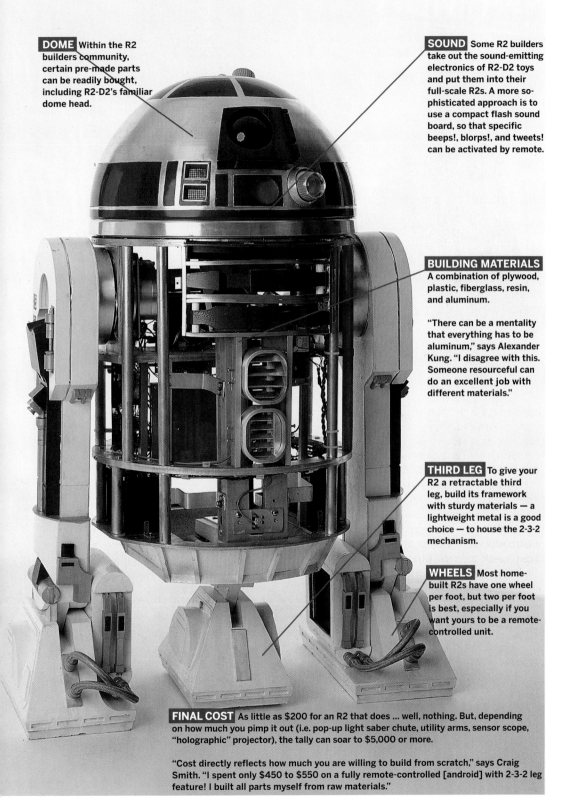

DOME Within the R2 builders community, certain pre-made parts can be readily bought, including R2-D2's familiar dome head.

SOUND Some R2 builders take out the sound-emitting electronics of R2-D2 toys and put them into their full-scale R2s. A more sophisticated approach is to use a compact flash sound board, so that specific beeps!, blorps!, and tweets! can be activated by remote.

BUILDING MATERIALS A combination of plywood, plastic, fiberglass, resin, and aluminum.

"There can be a mentality that everything has to be aluminum," says Alexander Kung. "I disagree with this. Someone resourceful can do an excellent job with different materials."

THIRD LEG To give your R2 a retractable third leg, build its framework with sturdy materials — a lightweight metal is a good choice — to house the 2-3-2 mechanism.

WHEELS Most home-built R2s have one wheel per foot, but two per foot is best, especially if you want yours to be a remote-controlled unit.

FINAL COST As little as $200 for an R2 that does ... well, nothing. But, depending on how much you pimp it out (i.e. pop-up light saber chute, utility arms, sensor scope, "holographic" projector), the tally can soar to $5,000 or more.

"Cost directly reflects how much you are willing to build from scratch," says Craig Smith. "I spent only $450 to $550 on a fully remote-controlled [android] with 2-3-2 leg feature! I built all parts myself from raw materials."

PRINTED CIRCUIT BOARDS

Step-by-step instructions for making your own PCBs at home. By Andrew Argyle

You can make a PCB for anything, even a headline.

Making your own printed circuit board (PCB) might seem a daunting task, but once you master the steps, it's easy to attain professional-looking results.

Printed circuit boards, which connect chips and other components, are what make almost all modern electronic devices possible. PCBs are made from sheets of fiberglass clad with copper, usually in multiple layers. Cut a computer motherboard in two, for instance, and you'll often see five or more differently patterned layers. Making boards at home is relatively easy, but limited to one- or two-layer designs. Here's how to create a one-layer board for a blinking LED circuit. For PCBs, this exercise is the equivalent of a beginner's "Hello World" program in software.

PCB
Make vs. Buy

Advantages of PCBs

Circuitry built on custom boards is sturdier, more stable, and more compact than the same electronics strung together by hand. And since it takes less time to assemble, PCBs are also better for making multiples. They're cheap and easy to prototype, and you can find a variety of templates and projects online.

You can order custom PCBs through design houses, but they are expensive — and the per-unit cost is especially high for small batches. Also, when you change the design, a shop will typically take several days to turn it around. Since it's normal for a board to go through several revisions, this adds up to a significant delay.

Process Overview

We'll design our printed circuit on the computer, as a plain black-and-white image. Black represents where we want the board to have copper connections between our circuit's components, while the white background corresponds to areas of plain, non-conducting fiberglass. Then we'll print the design onto special transparency film and iron it onto the copper side of a blank PCB (which starts out with copper completely covering one side). We peel the film back off, and the printed design remains on the copper. Next, the magic happens: when we bathe the board in an etching solution, copper dissolves away in the blank areas of our design, leaving conductive "traces" behind where we had drawn the circuit's connections. After this, we prepare the board for soldering, then finally go to town with the components.

Broken down step-by-step, the entire process can be summarized as follows:

1. **Create the design.**
2. **Print or photocopy the design.**
3. **Prepare the PCB.**
4. **Transfer the design to the copper.**
5. **Check and correct the traces.**
6. **Etch the board.**
7. **Clean and drill the board.**
8. **Solder the components.**

TIP: PCB design houses are well worth the price if you have a finished layout. But if your project is relatively simple, or the design is still evolving, then making your own PCB is the way to go.

MATERIALS:

TECHNIKS PRESS-N-PEEL PCB TRANSFER FILM (20 sheets for $30), *techniks.com*

AMMONIUM PERSULFATE CRYSTALS (1Kg for $20), *mgchemicals.com*

BLACK CORRECTION PEN (Lumocolor or fine-tip Sharpie)

PCB COPPER BOARD (9 x 12 x 0.062-inch, 1 oz., single-sided, $12), *techniks.com*

CIRCUIT COMPONENTS

TOOLS:

SCOURING PAD (do not use steel wool)

PHOTOCOPIER OR LASER PRINTER

ELECTRIC CLOTHES IRON

HARD WOODEN BOARD

LARGE POT AND PLASTIC TRAY for etching

HIGH-SPEED DRILL AND BITS

SOLDERING MATERIALS

PERF BOARD AND WIRE (OPTIONAL) for prototyping

NOTE: Techniks Press-n-Peel transfer film is a reasonable compromise between ease-of-use and cost. You could mask a board for etching with just a permanent marker, but this would take a long time, and it would be extremely difficult to make the lines sharp and accurate enough.

Photography by Andrew Argyle

START »

1. CREATE THE DESIGN

If you're building a circuit from scratch, rather than using a known design, you should prototype it first. One way is to string it up on a piece of perf board, as shown at right. Our "Hello World" blinker circuit has a 555 timer chip, a battery, a capacitor, an LED, and three resistors.

The underside of our proto-board is a "spaghetti patch" of wiring that will inevitably lead to problems. Even with this simple example, it's easy for wires to touch and short out. With all wires shielded, it's still ugly — inelegant and difficult to decipher and debug. This is a powerful reason for making a PCB.

Start with your circuit's schematic diagram, then lay out the PCB design based on the actual sizes of your components. You can create your design with any drawing, paint, or design program. I use EAGLE CadSoft (*www.cadsoft.de*), which is shareware.

First, produce your layout with components drawn in life-size. Print this out double-size for later reference. Then generate your final layout by removing the parts outlines.

You're designing the underside of the board, so your layout should be a mirror image of the arrangement you'd see looking from above. Also, you'll turn the printing to face the copper you're etching, so lettering should be backward.

Indicate parts placement and the location of Pin 1 on any chip. For future reference, you should also list the design's date and a revision number.

And with a small design, make multiple copies side-by-side; this increases the odds that at least one will work.

Prototype top.

Prototype bottom.

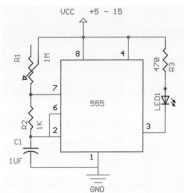
Schematic.

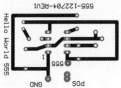
PCB with part placements.

PCB without part placements.

2. PRINT OR PHOTOCOPY THE DESIGN

Place the Techniks Press-n-Peel PCB transfer film in the tray of a laser printer or photocopier. One side of each sheet is shiny, while the other side is dull. Place the film so that the printing will come out on the dull side.

When using a laser printer, you want to minimize the possibility of damaging or curling the film. Use the "manual feed" feature to avoid making the film roll around the drum.

Once the film is printed, check it against a strong light for any defects. The film should be dark and no light should come through the traces.

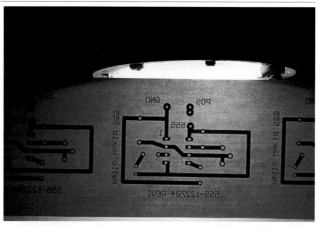

Checking for broken traces on the film.

3. CLEAN AND PREPARE THE PC BOARD

The PCB copper board should be as clean as possible so that the design adheres to it. Scrub it with dish soap and a scouring pad. Do not use steel wool, because it leaves tiny pieces of steel behind on the copper, which interfere with the etching.

Water should flow easily off the copper board. Dry the board to a polished finish with a lint-free cloth.

Cleaning the PCB.

You should use the board as soon as possible after cleaning, because otherwise the copper will begin to slowly oxidize in the air, diminishing its ability to take the design transfer and to etch well. Make sure not to touch the copper with bare hands.

NOTE: DO NOT TOUCH THE COPPER WITH YOUR BARE HANDS, SINCE SWEAT AND OIL LIKEWISE INTERFERE WITH THE TRANSFER AND ETCHING PROCESSES.

4. TRANSFER THE DESIGN TO THE COPPER

This is the most challenging step of making PCBs at home. First, cut the transparency to the same size as the PC board.

Find a fairly hard surface to iron on, such as a thick, wooden cutting board or a scrap piece of wood.

Set the iron to the polyester/rayon setting (medium heat on most irons). Once the iron has come up to temperature, lay it down directly on the wood to heat it. The warm wood will help with the adhesion and transfer of the film. Proper temperature control is critical; you will find it only through experimenting with your iron.

After about five minutes of warming the wood, lift the iron and lay the PCB down copper-side up. Align the film dull/printed-side down on the copper, and begin ironing firmly over the sheet, never lingering longer than four or five seconds in any one place. You want to avoid smearing the design.

Continue ironing for about 45 seconds, or longer if the copper board is thick. Then remove the board and let it air-cool, or cool it faster by putting it under cold water.

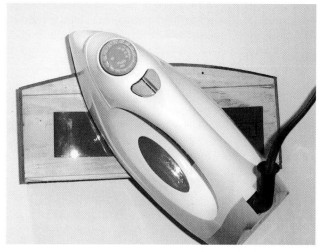

Ironing the PCB.

NOTE:
WARM THE IRONING SURFACE FOR FIVE MINUTES BEFORE IRONING THE PCB.

Settings:
SET IRON ON POLYESTER/ RAYON

Alignment:
CUT THE TRANSPARENCY TO THE SAME SIZE AS THE PC BOARD

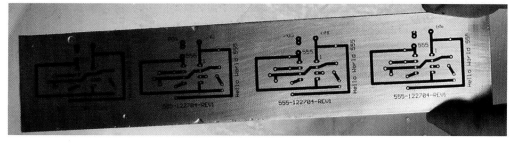

Cooled PCB board.

Carefully pull the film away from the board. If the design stays behind and appears on the copper, it's transferred successfully. Congratulations!

5. CHECK AND CORRECT THE TRACES

Examine the board for obvious errors. You can fix broken traces by filling in the gaps with a permanent marker such as a fine-tipped Sharpie. Use a hobby knife to separate any traces that have smeared together. Take the time to do a good, thorough job with this step, which can make or break your final product. For this reason, it's smart to print several designs, rather than pinning all of your odds on one.

6. ETCH THE BOARD

The chemicals used in etching are corrosive, and their fumes are irritating. Follow proper safety procedures, wear a mask (or work in a well-ventilated area), and protect your eyes.

There are different types of etching chemicals: dry and liquid. Dry chemicals are less expensive, but require dilution, as directed on the packaging. For this project, we recommend ammonium persulfate, available at lab and electronics supply stores. You will need about 1 quart of etching solution (etchant) to etch a 6" board.

Etching time is related to temperature. A small increase in temperature drastically reduces the time needed to etch a board, but too high a temperature makes the etchant too aggressive and gives off fumes. Aim for a temperature of around 125 degrees Fahrenheit (52°C).

Design houses have temperature-controlled etching tanks. For etching at home, you just need a stove, a large pot, and a plastic tray for the etchant.

Fill the pot halfway with water and heat to a simmer, but not a boil.

Put the PCB in the tray and place the tray on the simmering pot. Then slowly pour the etching solution into the tray.

The steam from the pot will slowly heat the etchant and increase the rate

Etch the PCB on the stove.

Etching in progress.

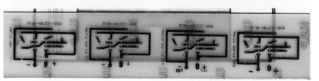
Etched PCB.

of etching. It should take no more than 15 to 30 minutes to do a proper etch. Gently agitate the tray during this time. This will remove bubbles, speed the etching, and make it more uniform. As shown in the middle picture on the facing page, you'll see copper dissolving away from the PC board.

When it cools, remove the board from the tray and thoroughly wash with water to remove all traces of the etchant. Wash again with a little dish soap to help neutralize any remaining acid.

7. CLEAN AND DRILL THE BOARD

Now the copper of the board has to be exposed for soldering. Use an abrasive pad or fine-grain (400 grit) sandpaper to scrub off the black film layer and reveal the copper underneath.

Etched and drilled board.

Drill the holes that the component leads fit into. If you're making many boards, it helps to use a drill press, or at least a power drill or Dremel, because hand-drilling can get tedious. The drill bits should have the same diameter as the etched holes.

Finally, if you repeated your design, cut the boards apart. Choose the best board to solder the components onto.

8. SOLDER

Use the double-sized parts placement diagram you printed earlier, and solder the parts into the PCB. If the board is an early revision, I always use sockets for any chips, as shown in the bottom photo, so I can remove them without having to desolder. If all is done right, then you've got a complete, functioning circuit on a beautiful little board.

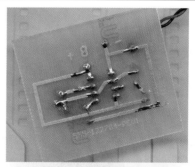

Underside of the completed board.

Homemade PCB blinkie circuit in operation.

FINISH ☒

Andrew Argyle (andrew@argyle.org) has been intrigued with electronics since taking apart his father's power tools. He is currently building Nixie clocks and etching mysterious projects somewhere in Canada.

BY SAUL GRIFFITH, NICK DRAGOTTA & JOOST BONSON
SPECIAL 'MALLOW THANKS TO JOEY McCUE & ERIC WILHELM

TUCKER

LEAVE *ME* ALONE!! I'M SHOOTING *THE BAD GUYS.*

HUH?

YOU'LL NEED THESE *GOGGLES* TO TAKE IT TO THE NEXT LEVEL.

OK, I'LL PLAY YOUR LITTLE GAME...

I'VE PUT THE SAFETY GLASSES ON. NOW WHAT?? *NOOOOOO!!!*

SAY *HELLO* TO MY LITTLE FRIEND! THE INFAMOUS *MARSHMALLOW SHOOTER.* I THOUGHT IT WAS ONLY POSSIBLE IN *THEORY!*

YOU THOUGHT WRONG.

YOUR ONLY MISTAKE WAS LETTING ME SEE IT!

USING MY PHOTOGRAPHIC MEMORY, I'LL MAKE AN EXACT REPLICA!!

YOU MAY HAVE *WON* THE *BATTLE*, BUT NOT THE *WAR!!*

HMMMPH!

I *HAD* NO IDEA *CELINE* WAS THIS *CLEVER*...

From the forthcoming book *HOWTOONS Book I* by Saul Griffith and Joost Bonsen. Published by arrangement with ReganBooks, an imprint of HarperCollins Publishers, Inc.

The best tools, software, gadgets, books, magazines, and websites.

TOOLBOX

Boblbee Megalopolis backpack
$189, www.boblbee.com

Keep your stuff safe beneath a shiny, high-impact plastic, injection-molded shell.

(Megalopolis Executive Spark shown)

I'm hard on gear. I drag my Power-Book, iPod, and digital camera everywhere I go. So over the years I've gone through a lot of bags and packs for storing gear.

The one pack I've found that serves all my needs is the Boblbee Megalopolis. It has a lightweight ergonomic ABS plastic outer shell that keeps my tech safe not only from the elements, but from direct impact. It also has a padded inner pocket that holds a 17-inch laptop. Because the laptop sits directly against the padded inner area that goes against the wearer's back, it's about as safe as it can be.

It also has connections for a variety of additional modules and holders. With a pair of side pockets and a bedroll strapped on, I can carry everything I need for a weekend trip. At $189, this may not be the cheapest option for lugging your gear, but it's certainly the most durable. And most of the parts are easily replaceable, including the outer shell. I've even modded mine so that I can plug all my gear into a power strip inside and simply plug in the pack itself at the end of my day.

—Josh Ellis

TIVO FOR RADIO

RadioSHARK
$70, griffintechnology.com

radioSHARK

I've been trying to figure out how to listen to "This American Life" on my iPod, without having to buy the episodes on Audible.com (too expensive). I tried Radio Recorder (xrl.us/radiorecorder) and AudioHijack (rogueamoeba.com), both of which allow you to record RealAudio streams, but I have bad luck with RealAudio — the stream hardly ever plays from start to finish, leaving me with an incomplete program.

Hopefully, I'll never have to open a RealAudio file again now that I've got a RadioSHARK. This is a real AM/FM radio that plugs into your computer's USB port.

(It gets its name from its shark-fin shape.) You tune the radio and schedule a recording by using the application that comes with the RadioSHARK. The application saves files as huge AIFFs or much smaller AACs — your choice.

Now I'm able to record "This American Life," "Science Friday," and "Fresh Air" and listen to them while I work out at the gym.

RadioSHARK is great to use live, as well. Like TiVo, you can pause live radio, rewind, and — if you've got enough of a program stored in the buffer — fast forward, too.

—Mark Frauenfelder

MAKE FAVORITE GADGET

iLife for Your TV

EyeHome
$149 refurbished, elgato.com

Elgato's EyeHome is my favorite new toy. It's fundamentally an iLife-to-audio-and-video converter: plug an ethernet cable into the "input" side of it, and then connect the A/V outputs of your choice (RCA-jack analog or SPDIF audio; video is composite, component, or S-Video) to your home theater system (in my case, a crappy TV and an ancient stereo). The EyeHome communicates (HTTP over port 8000) with an EyeHome server installed on a Mac in the network, requests content, and plays it back. It works just fine over 802.11g. The unit is tiny: 8"x8"x1½" and weighs less than a pound. And, because it's fanless, it's utterly silent.

The content it plays can be EyeTV-recorded TV shows, music from your iTunes library, video files, or photos from iPhoto albums. There's also a web browser of limited utility. For the things I most wanted to do with it — listen to music and watch movies — it works marvelously. I can hear some compression artifacts in the audio (a tinny high end and some overall murkiness), but it's still quite listenable. The picture viewer is at least as good as my DVD player's JPG viewer.

Its inability to play purchased iTunes Music Store tracks or Quick-Time movies is a bit distressing, but if you're willing to put up with some transcoding to get your video into MPEG or DivX format and your audio into something without DRM, it's not a big problem.

—Adam Thornton

Use EyeHome to send content from your Mac to your TV and stereo.

SOLDERING MADE SIMPLE

"Cold Heat" Soldering Iron
$20, radioshack.com and other sources

"As Seen on TV!" When shopping for quality electronics tools, that's the logo I look for. I was both intrigued and skeptical when I saw this marker-sized gadget in an electronics catalog, along with a brief description that indicated it soldered, while remaining cool to the touch, using just four AA batteries.

Of course, I had to take it apart to see what was inside. About what you'd expect for 20 bucks: some simple battery holders, snap-fit parts, etc. But, interestingly enough, it also contained a small circuit board complete with an IC that had obviously been "sterilized" by having its markings sanded off.

Equally interesting was the removable soldering tip. Apparently composed of a hard carbon compound, the tip is forked into two electrically isolated tines. To solder, the two tines are shorted across the joint. This allows a large current to flow across the "short," electrically heating it until it's hot enough to melt solder.

The combination of the mysterious circuit and the unusual tip do manage to slam a lot of current through the junction, as witnessed by the impressive spark you get when a good connection is made. Making that connection is critical to the process, and the iron has a dedicated LED that illuminates to indicate that you've hit the mark.

Does it work? Yeah, kinda. The Cold Heat iron seems best suited for small- to medium-sized connections that are mechanically solid and well supported. The pressure required to achieve and maintain a good electrical contact is considerably more than I was used to. I found myself chasing my victim components around the bench until I learned to lock them down before trying to solder them with the Cold Heat iron.

Bottom line: A good buy at the price and handy for your portable tool kit. Since it uses alkaline cells, it's always ready to go, unlike NiCad-powered irons I've owned, which seemed to alternate between dead-from-self-discharge and dead-from-overcharging with no stops in between. The Cold Heat iron is ready to solder quicker than a gas-powered iron, and it cools down seconds after use. If you need a portable iron, the Cold Heat is worth a look, but I wouldn't think of replacing my bench iron with it.

—*Bob Scott*

Tiptop Tips

Solder Tip Cleaning Genie
Part#156777, $5,
www.jameco.com

Man, do I love this thing! It's a metal, ashtray-like dish crammed with brass shavings that allows you to quickly and safely clean your iron's tip without lowering its temperature. All you do is stab the tip into the shavings to clean it.

It has reduced the amount of smoke my soldering generates, making me feel, after long soldering sessions, a lot less like I've got the mental acuity of Jessica Simpson. No brain-cell-loving solder-wielder should be without one.

—*Gareth Branwyn*

SONGS MADE SIMPLER
iPod Shuffle
$100, apple.com

I have about 1,000 vinyl albums, 600 CDs, and enough MP3 files to fill an 80-gig disk. Unfortunately, I have discovered that having music is not the same as listening to music. Like the 12-disc CD changer in my car that never gets changed, I always played the same handful of CDs. New titles would come in and old ones would leave, but my music collection and I had become strangers. Then I bought the iPod shuffle.

This tiny techno-goodie has reacquainted me with my music collection. I can pick from the full library or a specific playlist and then let iTunes generate a random

list to fit on my shuffle. I can also use the iTunes Smart playlist options to limit tracks to a certain genre. That way, the Beastie Boys and Winton Marsalis need never meet, unless I wish it.

I've heard the gripes about the lack of any kind of screen, and the fact that it only stores 1G of songs, but sometimes simpler is better. I find I spend less time fiddling about with what goes on my iPod shuffle because it's so easy to change. If the mix doesn't work, I generate a new random list of songs. I can pick if I want to, limit if I choose to, but most importantly, I have the option of simply choosing to listen to music.

That's the truly wonderful thing about the iPod shuffle; I spend less time picking songs and more time listening to music.

—John Clark

Just enough is more: limited features on the iPod Shuffle means less twiddling and more listening.

Pixel Papers
AvantGo.com, *free*
Palm Vx, *$40, used on eBay.com*

I've stopped buying newspapers. I read them on a Palm Vx running AvantGo. This old grayscale palmtop's screen has extremely good contrast and it's reflective. That means that reading it is like reading a book — if there's enough light to read a book, there's enough for the Palm Vx.

The AvantGo software is free if you download 3 MB of newspapers and magazines at a time. Or you can pay $15 a year to get 8MB of downloads. All you need to do is sync your Palm every morning for the current *New York Times, Guardian,* or whatever paper you've chosen, and you're ready for your subway commute.

—Aleks Oniszczak

DIY Cornucopia
 website

McMaster-Carr Online Catalog
www.mcmaster.com

McMaster-Carr is a hardware supply outfit that sells a bewildering variety of tools, equipment, and raw materials — plastics, metal stock, cable and wire, and rope — primarily to industry, but they do sell to individuals. It's the kind of thing that a serious DIY person should know about.

Their physical catalog is a giant, unwieldy, multi-volumed thing, but they've managed to get it all on their website. The website selections map to catalog pages. There's something sobering and wonderful about clicking on (say) "masking tape" and seeing that they have five pages of the stuff, beginning on page 3,199.

I've ordered from them several times without a hitch. Anecdotally, I've heard stories about items arriving with blinding speed.

—Stefan Jones

A BRIGHT, SHINY FUTURE
Future Floor Wax, *$6*

Johnson Wax sells Future as a floor polish, but it's really a clear acrylic paint. Put it on a clean, reasonably smooth, non-porous surface and that surface becomes shiny. I use it on model rockets, to protect the decals and make a slick aerodynamic finish, but you could use it on all sorts of projects.

Future thins and cleans up with water. I apply it with a slightly damp foam brush, but I've heard of people using it in an airbrush. It's best applied on hot, dry days; humidity causes it to fog up. Future cures hard enough for a new coat after a couple of hours. After a couple of days it dries hard enough to be buffed and polished with a clean, soft cloth.

—*Stefan Jones*

Robotics Resource
Servo Magazine
12 issues/$24.95, servomagazine.com

Over the years, there have been several attempts at creating a magazine aimed at robot enthusiasts. Sadly, none of them have been around for more than a few issues. So it was with great anticipation that we hobbyists awaited the release of *Servo*,

Bot-builder's bible

a robo-centric magazine spun off from the venerable *Nuts & Volts*.

Each issue strikes a deft balance of project-oriented pieces, articles that tackle more conceptual aspects of robotics, reviews of new hardware and software, introductions to different fields of robotics, how-tos for kids and newbies, and much more. Stand-out features include "Ask Mr. Roboto," Pete Miles's Q&A column, and the "Brain Matrix," a two-page comparison chart of different robot components (microcontrollers, gear motors, radio transceivers).

With so many awesome and affordable robotic parts, powerful microcontrollers, and open source software tools now available, coupled with internet communities to cross-pollinate cool hacks, the time seems perfect for a magazine that can take bottom-up bots to the next level. Let's hope *Servo* succeeds – we're keeping our end effectors crossed.

—*Gareth Branwyn*

MAKE SOFTWARE PICK

End the Drag of Dragging
Desktop Manager for OS X
Free, wsmanager.sourceforge.net

One thing that's always bugged me about graphic user interfaces is having to move the windows around. Over the last ten years I've come to accept it as a lousy inevitability of using a computer. But this annoyance vanished in one fell swoop after I installed Desktop Manager for Mac OS X. This free application lets you set up as many virtual desktops as you want, which you can access with keyboard commands, or by clicking little iconic representations of the desktops.

Now I have a desktop for blogging (with Safari and Ecto), a desktop for email (Mail and Safari), one for scheduling (iCal and Life Balance), and several others. I think of the program as a way to give me a giant display — albeit one that I can see only a section at a time. I can never go back to using my computer without this program.

—*Mark Frauenfelder*

RSS Anywhere
Bloglines.com

As the number of online news sources grows, keeping current becomes difficult. An RSS client helps organize the mess.

But if you want to read your feeds anywhere, you have to either set up another client, or resort to the "old-fashioned" way of visiting the sites.

Bloglines lets you stay current wherever you may be. The web-based service acts like any aggregator but can be accessed online. With Bloglines, staying current on dozens of news feeds is as easy as checking your email.

—Zach Slootsky

Everlasting Sandpaper

Mylar Backed Sanding Film
$1.69 per sheet

This stuff has been around forever, but few people seem to know about it. It's like sandpaper, but the abrasives are based on a plastic film. You can roll it, fold it, and wet-sand with it without ruining the sheet or causing grit to get all over your work. I wash sheets that have become clogged or dirty in my kitchen sink. Heavy use makes the stuff more flexible and finer; I have comfortable old scraps in my toolbox that I've been using for five years. The extra-fine varieties can be used to smooth and polish plastic and certain types of paint finishes.

You'll find sanding film in craft or hobby stores; it comes in small (typically 4"x5½") sheets in a variety of grits. Several brands are available. The ones I've seen most often include Flex-I-Grit (by K&S Engineering) and Super Film (by Houston Art, Inc.).

—Stefan Jones

GROOVY GRAMOPHONES

Berliner Gramophone Kit and Edison Cylinder Kit, by Gakken
approximately $40 each, imported through HobbyLink Japan, www.hlj.com

These kits are part of a Japanese series of assembly-required, "adult-education" models. The functioning Edison Cylinder and Berliner Gramophone kits offer the allure of carving grooves into compact discs and Dixie cups.

Both kits have a sewing-needle-based pickup and playback assembly, and are constructed from a motor and various bits of wood, plastic, and Styrofoam. Gakken has provided thoroughly illustrated instructions in both Japanese and surprisingly well-translated English. The assembly of each kit takes about an hour and only requires a screwdriver, some scotch tape, and a battery.

Once assembled, it's relatively simple to start recording. On both kits, flipping a switch starts the motor spinning; then you speak into a cup for between 30 and 60 seconds. The cup is directly attached to the needle, which scratches a linear representation of the sound into either a CD or a plastic cup. To play back the recording, the needle rides in the freshly scratched grooves, and the vibrations are transmitted to the cup, producing audible playback.

The Gramophone kit seems to be the most 'show-offable' bang for your buck, though both kits do a fine job of delivering an archaic, hands-on audio experience. Recommended for all ages.

—Adam W. Kempa

FILLER UP

Elmer's Wood Filler
$2 for an 8-ounce tub

I build a lot of models from balsa and basswood. These are grainy, porous woods that soak up paint and look awful unless filled and sanded. I've tried a lot of fillers through the years, and they've all lacked something. Some require many coats. Others are a bear to sand. The best I've found is Elmer's Wood Filler. It can fill the grain of most woods with one coat, dries quickly, sands beautifully, and takes paint nicely.

You can find this versatile stuff in almost any hardware store. It comes in light and dark color varieties, in small and large tubs. It's water-based, fairly benign, and easy to handle. I've used it out of the tub as a gap-filling putty and thinned down as a brush-on filler.

—Stefan Jones

Elmer knows how to make cheap wood look good.

Call Your Attention to Order

NADH (2.5mg)
$19 for 30 tablets, widely available at health-food stores

To call whatever my problem is "attention deficit disorder" probably does a grave disservice to medically distracted persons everywhere, but I've known for years now that something's definitely up with my brain. I wish I had a satisfying polysyllabic shingle for my hang-up, but all I know is that coffee helps a little and ephedrine used to help a lot.

Of course, those spineless wingnuts at the FDA allowed 150 Darwinist case studies to ruin it for everyone, so now no one is getting anything done. Thanks a lot, stroke-disposed college freshmen!

NADH (Nicotinamide Adenine Dinucleotide) definitely helps me concentrate appropriately, and I have no idea why. I take one tablet of this conenzyme on rising and another half an hour before lunch, and so far, over two months, the results have been salutary. You don't get those intriguing shakes, but there's a calm feeling of readiness that can be very reassuring. I also have the sense that I'm remembering to pause, reflect,

and focus more readily than I've typically done in the past. Very much more.

Maybe this newfound dearth of spazziness is a natural consequence of turning 38, but until they can get that sad eventuality into a gelcap, I give my hearty and unqualified okey-dokey to this weird mystery enzyme.

—Merlin Mann

Power Panel

Viewsonic Airpanel V110
$400 refurbished, check Froogle.com

I have a wireless network, a PocketPC, and an old Vadem Clio 1050 with a wireless card. But the PocketPC's screen is too small for more than occasional viewing, and the Clio is stuck with an old version of Internet Explorer (I couldn't even log into Amazon). I had been searching online for a tablet PC when I stumbled across something called a "Smart Display" — in this particular instance, a refurbished Airpanel.

It's basically a dumb terminal with built-in Wi-Fi and a touchscreen running Windows CE. After fiddling a bit to get it set up, it worked like a charm, and now I wonder how I got along without it. It allows you complete access to your home PC's desktop and all the applications and data stored therein. The extra bonus? By running Windows CE, not XP, it's an instant-on machine.

In the kitchen, I can call up my recipe box on Epicurious.com; in the family room, I can post to my blog while catching up with CSI; and, in the living room, I can show off vacation photos. How on earth did I survive without it?

—Adam Bernard

Watts Happening?
18watt.com

18watt.com started as a Yahoo group for people interested in a rare Marshall guitar amp made in the 1960s. People shared details of the circuit and design.

There are now companies offering kits and complete amplifiers based on 18watt. com's research. (Marshall reissued the amp, bringing the whole deal full circle.)

At 18watt.com, folks with a little electrical know-how can make, for about $500, an amp that could otherwise cost $7,000 for an original.

—John Irvine

DESTROY

To Make You've Got to Destroy

Spyderco Endura
$73, spyderco.com

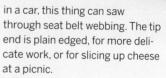

It's inevitable: at least once a day you're going to have to ruin someone else's handiwork. You've got to cut some rope, open a packing box, delicately cut a printed circuit board trace, and to do all of these things and more, you'll need a knife. My knife of choice is the Spyderco Endura. Unless I'm traveling by air, this thing is always in my pocket.

Why Spyderco? Of the bewildering array of knife manufacturers, they've always merged high concept with low tech. Spyderco knives offer easy one-handed opening

thanks to the hole in the blade.

In the knife world, where claims of "the official knife of the Navy SEALS" are used to push Rambo-sized bayonets and barely legal "automatic" knives, the Endura is a model of simplicity. The handle is tough but lightweight fiber-glass-reinforced nylon, pebbled so your grip won't slip. The handiest form of the blade is half-serrated and half-plain. The serrations might look mean, but they're quite handy — the serrated half is nearest the handle, for tougher cutting jobs. If you're trapped

in a car, this thing can saw through seat belt webbing. The tip end is plain edged, for more delicate work, or for slicing up cheese at a picnic.

Not counting the clip, the Endura is only ⅜" thick, with a blade almost four inches long. If the Endura looks like too much knife for you, try its little brother, the Delica model.

—Richard Butner

Fossilize Your Cardboard

Minwax High Performance Wood Hardener
$16 for a pint-size can

This is as much an invitation to experiment as a review.

Minwax Wood Hardener is an obnoxious-smelling, toxic, flammable, watery-thin fluid used to treat weathered or rotten window frames and door sills. It's essentially a deep-penetrating liquid plastic. It binds together wood fibers, replacing the natural lignin "glue."

It works as advertised, but I, and others in the rocket-nerd community, have found some additional applications. When applied to fresh, new wood, it creates a hard, dent-resistant, water-resistant surface that (when thoroughly dry) sands very nicely. It also seals the wood grain, meaning you'll need less paint or stain when finishing porous wood.

Cardboard and cardstock soaked in the stuff become hard, rigid, and water resistant; the resulting material resembles phenolic plastic and can be sanded and machined with power tools.

Some hints: Never work with this stuff indoors! The solvent in Minwax Wood Hardener is vile stuff. Use a disposable brush, containers you don't mind throwing away, and wash your hands afterwards.

Porous woods expand a bit with Wood Hardener. Treating only one side of a piece of wood may cause it to warp.

Initial sanding of treated pieces may be difficult because Minwax strengthens the wood's surface "fuzz." After an initial smoothing, however, you'll have a surface that can be wet-sanded to a high polish.

—Stefan Jones

Double your connections, double your audio fun.

PLUGS-A-PLENTY

Piggyback Audio Cables
$10, radioshack.com

My preamp mixer has too much stuff plugged into it. A pair of turntables, laptop PC, and portable CD player consume the four stereo inputs. Then there's the radio signal from my stereo amplifier, my MiniDisc recorder/player, and occasionally, various other devices with an audio out, like my Game Boy Advance SP. Plugging and unplugging isn't a valid option in the long run, and not just because it's a hassle. A limited number of inputs requires me to plan in advance what I want to use. Furthermore, you inflict damage on those plugs each time you yank them free, stretching the connector and loosening the wiring.

So, what's a sound addict to do? Well, you can rig a reverse-splitter, but there's a more elegant solution: killer, gold-plated "piggy-back" audio cables (catalog #42-2620 at RadioShack, but other variations are out there). They replace one of your standard audio cables with a set that allows for a second simultaneous input. The piggybacks look weird at first, like those mutant toads that grow downriver from nuclear power plants, but they efficiently double the number of inputs to your mixer or stereo. And, yes, you can piggyback a piggyback, but doing so welcomes sound degradation.

—Marc Weidenbaum

Bottle Rocket

Cork Pop III
$28, corkpops.com and amazon.com

If you find yourself putting a wine bottle between your legs and tugging an old-fashioned corkscrew to pull out a cork, here's a new twist on wine openers: the Cork Pop III. This wine opener uses a low-pressure propellant cartridge to blast the cork from the bottle. Cork Pop III houses a needle that you insert all way through the

cork; then you press the cartridge to release a jet of air and ... lift off. The cork doesn't fly through the air but you can imagine that it does. Getting the cork off the needle is the only difficulty I've had using it.

A cartridge will open about 60-80 bottles before you need a refill. Amazon reviewer, Leanna J. Kamp, said she used up her cartridge because she liked teasing her bird who whistled when it heard the blast of air.

—Dale Dougherty

Repairs by the Roll

Gaffer's Tape
$16 a roll, thetapeworks.com

Many people swear by duct tape for all their taping needs, but I think its adhesive is too gummy, its backing is too plasticy, its fabric is too difficult to tear, and it tastes bad. (If you don't know how your tape tastes, you've obviously never hung from a catwalk with one hand while securing a bundle of wires with the other hand and tearing the tape with your teeth.)

I prefer gaffer's tape. Gaffers are the people on a film crew responsible for stringing cables around, and this tape is designed to hold equipment securely and remove cleanly. It doesn't dry out like duct tape, and it doesn't leave adhesive residue on most surfaces. The fabric backing of gaffer's tape tears easily and doesn't tend to split lengthwise like duct tape seems to do at the worst moments. It's also not as vinyl-like as duct tape, so it provides a better gripping surface and doesn't smell like a Datsun interior. It typically comes in black and white as well as standard gray, and some suppliers

provide it in a variety of useful colors, including Chroma-Key blue and green, for those digital video effects projects of yours.

Gaffer's tape is noticeably more expensive than duct tape, but all quality tools are pricier than their generic counterparts.

I use it for running cables along paint and carpet, repairing electrical wiring, temporary fabric mending, and ruggedizing the broken spines of my favorite softcover reference books. It's thick enough to be opaque in most light, so I also use it for covering the ads on the spines of my telephone directories.

—Elliott C. "Eeyore" Evans

Have you used something worth keeping in your toolbox? Let us know at *toolbox@makezine.com.*

John Irvine sings and plays guitar with The Jennifers (*thejennifers.com*) in Baltimore, MD. ... **Elliott C. "Eeyore" Evans** posts descriptions of his projects at *www.ee0r.com/proj* ... **Joshua Ellis** is a writer, musician, and co-founder of Mperia.com ... **Stefan Jones** dabbles in net-futurism, model

rocketry, and gaming ... **Richard Butner** is a writer and technology consultant in Raleigh, N.C. ... **John Clark** is a web programmer (*webwork.12ftguru.com*) ... **Adam Kempa** documents his latest nerdly pursuits at *Kempa.com* ... **Marc Weidenbaum** (*disquiet.com*) writes and edits, with an emphasis on electronic music and comic books ... **Adam Bernard** is an auto industry analyst by day and a gadget freak by

night ... **Merlin Mann** helps people make interesting things for the Global Interweb ... **Aleks Oniszczak** is finishing his masters in human-computer interaction ... **Gareth Branwyn** is cyborg-in-chief at Street Tech (*www.streettech.com*) ... **Zach Slootsky** is a computer science student at the University of Toronto ... **Adam Thornton** is a bewhiskered curmudgeon.

✳ I made the Steadicam while I was up in northern Minnesota at my girlfriend's family's house. Her dad had a drill press and we bought all the parts at a local Minard's hardware store. He and I put it together in an amazingly short amount of time, and it really works well with the larger camcorders like my Panasonic DVX-100a. Following Johnny Lee's advice on his website, we made a sled for extra support. Really good bang for the buck. And so easily transportable ... broke it down and brought it all back to New York in an already-full duffle bag.
— *Derek Wang*

✻ I just got the first issue (of many) of MAKE, and man I LOVE it! I'm one of those odd people. I've been in the computer industry, at all levels, for 20 years. I'm an amateur scientist working in electronics, physics, and cosmology. You have succeeded in putting together a magazine that appeals to just about every one of my interests, and that, sir, is no small feat. Congratulations and keep the breadth of articles coming!

I do have one request. On the computer articles, I noticed that they were a bit heavy on the Mac side. Hey, somebody should be. But I would like it if some references were made in each of these articles to PC versions of the hardware or software, not complete rewrites, just an annotation. The same should be done for the Macs when the article is PC-dominated. Of course, both should also include Linux references as well. Thanks again.

—Hunter N. Kelley

✻ I just got my copy of MAKE that you sent. I got goose bumps. This is a very important magazine. It reminds me of what I used to read as a kid: *Popular Electronics*. That got me going way back then, and I'd count the days until each issue came. I learned of the new thing, integrated circuits, from there. I built Heathkits, etc., etc., and got started on my life as an engineer. We know what it did for Gates and Allen. I think this will be just as important. It isn't doing all the projects as much as reading about them and then finally making a move yourself.

Many a parent will get the next generation of engineers going by doing some of these projects with their kids or even reading it with them. I just wanted to give you a congratulations and thank you since I smile so much when I thumb through it. May it sell millions of copies! —*Dan Bricklin*

✻ When I went out to my car this morning, there was a MAKE magazine subscription card tucked under the windshield. Telstar Logistics has been outed. —*Todd Lappin*

(*Editor's note: Todd Lappin is the author of* Urban Camouflage, *MAKE, Volume 01.*)

✻ Just got my first issue of MAKE and devoured it in about 90 minutes. Very nice work. I have a feeling I'll read it like I read *National Geographic Adventure*: as a means of satisfying that urge to do something I know I'll never get off my ass and actually do.

—*Jeremy Lyon*

✻ Suggestions for the Magazine:

1. Put MAKE's URL on the outside cover, or at least somewhere in the table of contents. Anything so no one else (besides me) wastes their time typing in makejournal.com and getting nowhere.:)

2. Don't use Movable Type. Use WordPress, and then you won't need Ecto (page 147). The very phrase "Blogging made simple" sounds like "Breathing made simple."

Well, I have to go read about the backyard monorail now. Oh, and I really like the home linear acceleratorette. Nice job! —*Genny Engel*

✻ I've not yet received my copy of MAKE. As a result, I'm feeling inadequate and unloved. Others are mocking me and refusing to let me peek over their shoulders while they revel in the luscious goodness of their copies. When I walk into a room, they're reduced to furtive glances, snickering, whispered conversations, and some not-so-subtle fingerpointing. They signal each other by using this gangsta-like hand gesture. Please rescue me from this hellish state. —*Eldon Sprickerhoff*

(*Editor's note: This letter was received in early March. We quickly rectified the situation.*)

Talk to us about past volumes of MAKE, story and project ideas, or other things you think the readers of MAKE should know about, at makezine.com/talk.

Make: Amends

In Volume 01, *Toolbox* section, the Kroll tailcap switch discussed will, in fact, not work on the L4 Digital Lumamax. Here's what will work: the Aleph tailcap ($45), available at OSCommerce (www.oreilly.com/go/aleph) or the McE2S LOTC two-stage switch DIY Kit ($30, lets you mod the stock switch to give two light levels), available at www.oreilly.com/go/mce2skit.

In Volume 01, *Made on Earth* section, we inadvertently put Case Western Reserve University in Pennsylvania instead of Cleveland, Ohio, where it has thrived since 1826.

Q: What's cooler than a MAKE T-shirt?
A: A MAKE T-shirt you got free by being the first person to point out a glaring technical error in this or upcoming volumes! Send them on to editor@make.com.

The Laptop That Wouldn't Say Die

Twenty-two years later, people still love the TRS-80 Model 100.

EVER TAKE YOUR LAPTOP ROCK CLIMBING?
In college, I often enjoyed hiking up to St. Anthony's Nose outside Easton, Penn. I'd find a nice spot in the woods and sit down with a book and my PowerBook to take notes. But battery life was very limited and I never felt comfortable setting my expensive, fragile laptop down in the dirt.

Eventually, I found a computer far more suited to my needs: the TRS-80 Model 100, built by Tandy Radio Shack in 1983. I paid $15 for a stack of three at the Trenton Computer Festival in 1998. You can get one on eBay for about $30. The Model 100 is a rugged little computer with a full-sized keyboard and a 40x8 character display. It powers on instantly and will run for 20 hours on 4 AA batteries. I can throw the Model 100 down in the dirt, leave it there running while I read, then pick it up and resume taking notes right where I left off.

The Model 100's built-in text editor is rudimentary, but adequate. Transferring files back to a modern computer is simple. Connect the Model 100 to your desktop system using a generic serial cable and a null modem adapter (RadioShack, $7). If your PC doesn't have a serial port, you'll also need a USB-to-serial adapter.

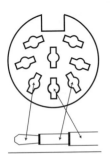

Mobile as modem: phone port to sub-mini jack.

With the systems connected, run TELCOM on the Model 100. Press F2 for "Stat" and type "88N1E" (9600 baud, 8 bits, no parity, 1-stop bit, enable flow control). Launch a terminal app on your desktop, configure it to the same settings, and enable automatic line feeds. Now you're ready to go. Press F4 for "Term" on the Model 100 and ensure your desktop is also in terminal mode. You can now transfer files using the Down/Up menus on the Model 100 and the "Capture Text" and "Send Text" options on your desktop.

This functionality served me well in college, but today my work revolves far more around email and the Unix command line than it does writing papers, which got me thinking about remote connectivity. The Model 100 has a built-in modem with an interesting feature — sound in/out lines for an acoustic coupler. These lines are intended for a telephone handset, but mightn't they work just as well with a cellular phone headset? The typical cellphone headset uses a 3/32" sub-mini phone jack (RadioShack, $3). Wire this to the Model 100's phone port; 14 AWG copper wire fits perfectly into its sockets.

Ensure the switches on the side of the Model 100 are set to ACP and ORIG, set Stat to M8N1E, and enter terminal mode. The system will seemingly freeze up as it waits for a connection. Dial the Club 100 BBS (925-939-1246) on your cellphone. At the modem tone, connect the phone to the computer. You'll see the login message. Congratulations!

You can also set up your own BBS. Connect a compatible modem, such as the US Robotics Courier (all versions), to your Mac OS X or *nix system, and enable dial-up connections. You now have access to every file on your computer (including email and Lynx) from any place you can get a cellphone connection. Practical applications abound for a cellphone-equipped Model 100. Suppose, for example, that while hiking in a remote region, you fall and break your larynx. With the TRS-80, you'll be able to email for help.

Tom Owad (owad@applefritter.com) is a Macintosh consultant in York, Penn., and editor of Applefritter (*applefritter.com*). He is the author of *Apple I Replica Creation* (Syngress, 2005).

Photograph by Tom Owad

THE LAST GENERATION OF ENGINEERS

Why digital rights management kills innovation.

AT THE ELECTRONIC FRONTIER FOUNDATION, part of my job is attending standards body meetings where they're hammering out agreements on Digital Rights Management (DRM), the technology used to restrict how you use the media you buy.

The idea is that when you buy a TV, a PVR, a CD player, or an eBook reader, the device will be slave to the whims of the entertainment industry. With DRM, a digital book will be set up to keep you from using it in any way not authorized by the publisher. Want to copy some text for your sig file? Loan it to a friend? Move it to a PDA? Tough. You'll have to shell out more money to do less. Consider how cellphone users get tricked into buying stripped-down versions of their favorite music to play as ringtones. If you already own the MP3, why should you have to buy the ringtone?

This is bad enough, but there's an even bigger downside for hardware hackers likely to buy an

> "Computer companies let entertainment companies tell them how to build PCs."

issue of MAKE: these things come with a requirement that the players be tamper resistant. For the first time, hardware vendors are required to make their A/V equipment — and components, like hard drives, video cards, and FireWire interfaces — resistant to attempts by end-users (that's you) to understand them, modify them, and improve them.

Worst of all is that the entertainment companies are buying laws, like the FCC's Broadcast Flag, to make it illegal for anyone to make a player that can be modified by users.

Back to the standards body meetings. They're full of engineers and lawyers. The lawyers usually can't see anything wrong with a world where their employers sell you your media one feature at a time: 20 bucks for a video, another buck for a

pause button, and 50 cents for a fast-forward. But the engineers really get to me. At a meeting in Edinburgh, this engineer who is a really nice guy was showing off the electronics kit he'd bought for his seven-year-old. "It's a far cry from the cat's whiskers and crystals my grandfather and I used to build radios," he said, reminiscing with the other engineers, most of whom had at one time built a tuner out of parts just to see how it was done.

This engineer was a participant in a standards-setting process for digital television. As part of this standard, it is assumed that it will be illegal for anyone to build a digital television tuner unless they're working for an approved company and they promise to lock up the results in epoxy, obfuscated code, and solder. Today you can build a really cool DTV tuner out of software and an analog-to-digital converter using the tools in the GNU Radio project (gnu.org/software/gnuradio). But under the rules these guys are helping to bring about, GNU Radio would be illegal.

This engineer — he's a skilled, passionate geek. He got to be that way when his grandpa showed him how to build a crystal tuner. But he'll never sit down with his own granddaughter and teach her how to hack a DTV tuner.

The computer companies at these meetings have sold us down the river. You've got about a year before the FCC makes GNU Radio illegal. Use it wisely. Go teach some kid to make a tuner. It might be the last chance you get.

Cory Doctorow (*craphound.com*) is European Affairs Coordinator for the Electronic Frontier Foundation (*eff.org*), a co-editor on Boing Boing (*boingboing.net*), and an award-winning science fiction writer (*craphound.com/est*). He lives in London, England.

MakeShift

By William Lidwell

The Scenario: It is easy to forget that access to potable water is considered a luxury for much of the world. You are reminded of this fact on a trip to a rural village in East Asia. You learn from the locals that their water supply has been contaminated — the cause of recent illnesses that sound a lot like cholera and dysentery. In addition to dirt, sewage, bacteria, and parasites, you suspect other contaminants such as arsenic and benzene from industrial dumping many miles up river. Ideally, nobody should drink this water — but the villagers are unwilling to relocate.

The Challenge: Create a makeshift solution to filter and purify the water. The solution should be permanent and able to provide drinkable water for 20 to 30 people. Tools and materials at your disposal include materials that can be reasonably extracted from the environment and items on the supply list. You have 48 hours.

Supply List:

- 2 barrels
- 1 bicycle with flat tires
- 1 car battery
- 6 one-liter plastic bottles of water
- Various lengths of bamboo tubes (1"-3" diameter)
- Variety of tools (saw, hammer, pliers, hand drill)
- Steel wool
- Endless supply of coconuts
- $10 in mixed American coins

Email a detailed description of your MakeShift solution with sketches and/or photos to makeshift@makezine.com by July 1. If duplicate solutions are submitted, the winner will be determined by the quality of the explanation and presentation. The most plausible and most creative solutions will win a MAKE T-shirt. Think positive and include your shirt size and contact information with your description. Good luck! For readers' solutions to previous MakeShift challenges, visit *makezine.com/makeshift*.

William Lidwell is a consultant with Stuff Creators Design Studio and co-author of the book *Universal Principles of Design*.

MAKER
Solving problems, fulfilling wishes.
CHALLENGE

Do you find yourself wishing for a dream machine or a system to solve a problem? Tell us about it. And if you have a good solution to one of the challenges submitted below, tell us about that, too. Send your stuff to challenge@makezine.com. We can't print all of the solutions here, so make sure you check out our website, makezine.com/challenge, for even more solutions.

Thumb Keys » I loved the thumb keys on my Kinesis Ergo keyboard. The thumb could hit six keys, including Ctl, Alt, Del, Home, End, Pg Up, Pg Down, Space, Enter.

The rest of the keyboard's features were superfluous to me. As I sit here with my standard keyboard, I really wish I could have a thin strip of keys mounted right below the space key so I could put Ctl and Alt down there for each thumb.

I'd be really happy if I could hack some switches right into the keyboard itself. But I'd also settle for some sort of USB interface that I could configure as keyboard keys in Linux.

Seems to me like it should be really simple yet very, very useful. Can anyone out there help me with this?
—Monty Zukowski

Dull the Hum » I have a resonance in my hot water heating system that causes an annoying humming in one part of the house whenever the circulator pump is running. This type of noise would be very easy to null out using the same type of system that is in the cheap noise-canceling headphones.

The idea would be to mount a speaker driver on the pipe and have the system cancel out the noise at the source. I'm sure there would be many similar applications.
—Christopher Johnson

Cat 5 Cable Continuity Tester » I often build or repair category 5 cables at home but do not have a continuity tester. Most of the ones I have seen on the market cost more than $50. Testers I have used in the past have 16 LEDs, 8 for each of the RJ45 connectors. A push button moves the voltage from pin 1 to pin 8 with each push. The LED on the source pin lights as well as the pin the signal arrives on, if the cable is built correctly.

This seems like a simple challenge for someone who knows what types of IC would help solve this problem.
—Todd Edmands

Dog Bark Stopper » I know they sell dog-barking stoppers, and I have tried three different ones of varied price (up to $75) and intensity. They are between 20-22 kHz in frequency. They work if the dog is close by.

I need one that is more direct, such as a small speaker placed in a tube to act like a rifle for direction. Would that be a project that you would like to undertake?
—Jack Russ

Chess Clock » For chess lovers, the price of chess clocks is ridiculous. Surely, there is a low-cost solution for those of us who would like to try Speed Chess and hone our skills for tournament play.
—John Bobo

Balloon Wi-Fi Antenna » I was thinking of trying to use a kite or balloon for a Wi-Fi antenna. What I wanted to do was make it in the shape of the Testors' Area 51 flying saucer: galacticvoyager.com/mod/area51/icon.gif.

Any ideas on the legality of using a balloon for Wi-Fi or any other valuable input for attempting this project?
—Todd Livingstone

HTPC Control from Universal Remote » I have a Home Theatre PC (HTPC) and would like to control it from a standard TV universal remote control. Is there a way to build/buy an IR detector that can be configured from the PC to recognize my remote's signals and to control iTunes, Windows Media Player, BSPlayer, Firefox, etc.?
—Mike Parker

Time Expansion Bat Detector » Design/create a homemade "time expansion" bat detector — very expensive to buy, but the best type to "see" the actual ultrasonic signal. There are schematics/plans available for "frequency division" detectors from scratch and hetrodyne detectors by converting an old radio. I once saw an "idea" mooted for a time division detector using a PIC, but it was not followed through.
—C. Payne

Wire My House Efficiently » I would like MAKE to solve a problem for me: I would like to know the best way to wire my house with a single wire type that can provide high-speed data and 12/5 DC volt power, in a single inexpensive plug.
—Timothy Hirzel

Math Money Machine » I'd like to see someone invent a "math money machine" which spews out coins when students solve math questions on a USB connected personal computer. A video explaining the concept is found at mathmoneymachine. blogspot.com.
—Phil Shapiro

Portable Dishwasher? » I live in an apartment in Brooklyn with a tiny kitchen. My girlfriend and I cook a lot, but we always have a problem with all the dishes we have to clean by hand. I think there ought to be a portable dishwasher that I can stow away under the sink when not in use.

If you like that one, I have another I thought up while writing a treatment for a TV show: a specially configured record player that plays digital files from vinyl records (MP3 Phonograph).
—Steven Swiller

ANSWERS TO PREVIOUS CHALLENGES:

Super 8 Film to DVD » In *Maker Challenge*, Gary Peare asked for a "really high-quality way to transfer old movies to digital at home." In our contest, "Mach flott den Schrott" (not translatable), see slashdot.org/article. pl?sid=05/02/08/0015242&tid=222&tid=126, Frank Kempelmann built a machine to transfer Super 8 films to his PC picture by picture: www.heise.de/ct/machflott/projekte/55840. It earned him the first prize.
—Johannes Endres

Inexpensive Way to Track Pets » Falconers and model rocketers use small transmitters. Here's a discussion: reality.sgiweb.org/overby/rockets/Beacons/.
—Gerald Woodard

Volume 02, May 2005. MAKE is published quarterly by O'Reilly Media, Inc. in the months of February, May, August, and November. O'Reilly Media is located at 1005 Gravenstein Hwy North, Sebastopol, CA 95472. (707) 827-7000. SUBSCRIPTIONS: Send all subscription requests to MAKE, P.O. Box 17046, North Hollywood, CA 91615-9588 or subscribe online at makezine.com/offer or via phone at 866-289-8847 (U.S. and Canada); all other countries call 818-487-2037. Subscriptions are available for $34.95 for 1 year (4 quarterly issues) in the U.S.; Canada: $39.95 USD; all other countries: $49.95 USD. Application to mail at Periodicals Postage Rates is pending at Sebastopol, CA, and at additional mailing offices. POSTMASTER: Send address changes to MAKE, P.O. Box 17046, North Hollywood, CA 91615-9588.

By Chris Smith

A NEW BREED OF ALCHEMISTS has discovered a way to make gaming gold and sell it for real money online. Players "farm" characters to get in-game items and resources and then sell them on the web. And a surprising economy is growing. One leading indicator is visible on eBay, which periodically shuts down these auctions for dealing in intellectual property. However, we saw plenty of people go for the gold in one of the hottest Massively Multiplayer Online Role-Playing Games, **World of Warcraft (WoW)**, by Blizzard Entertainment. World of Warcraft claimed 1.5 million subscribers worldwide just four months after its release. **In three months, there were $1,288,938 in eBay sales of WoW gold**, and the top seller in that period accumulated $111,404 in real cash.

FEB '05
TOTAL SALES:
$527,127

OTHERS
61%

TOP 5 SELLERS
21%
($111,482)

TOP SELLER
8%
($43,685)

TOP SELLERS: In February 2005, the top seller accounted for 8% of the sales on 1,261 listings and had an 85% success rate.

Dec '04	Jan '05	Feb '05
$241,905	**$519,906**	**$527,127**
Avg. price: $36.27	Avg. price: $44.22	Avg. price: $44.16
Listings: 13,598	Listings: 22,506	Listings: 18,081
Success rate: 46.4%	Success rate: 49.8%	Success rate: 63.7%

REVENUE GROWTH: WoW gold sales on eBay jumped from $241K in December to $519K in January, followed by a slight bump to $527K in February.

In February the average sale price was $.33 per unit of gold.

Nearly 60% of all listings were for 100 gold pieces.

Gold must be purchased for the specific server used by the player.

PRICES FOR SPECIFIC AMOUNTS OF GOLD

Based on February 2005 data, the best value is 400 gold pieces at 30 cents per piece. All quantities are in gold pieces.

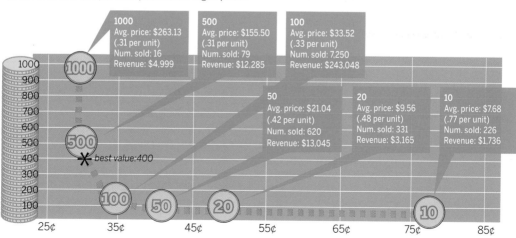

1000
Avg. price: $263.13
(.31 per unit)
Num. sold: 16
Revenue: $4,999

500
Avg. price: $155.50
(.31 per unit)
Num. sold: 79
Revenue: $12,285

100
Avg. price: $33.52
(.33 per unit)
Num. sold: 7,250
Revenue: $243,048

50
Avg. price: $21.04
(.42 per unit)
Num. sold: 620
Revenue: $13,045

20
Avg. price: $9.56
(.48 per unit)
Num. sold: 331
Revenue: $3,165

10
Avg. price: $7.68
(.77 per unit)
Num. sold: 226
Revenue: $1,736

best value: 400

25¢   35¢   45¢   55¢   65¢   75¢   85¢

Chris Smith is director of Business Development at Terapeak, which provided the data for this column. Chris can be reached at chris@terapeak.com.

My Atari 2600 Portable

By Benjamin J. Heckendorn

Items such as the bulky metal box RF modulator (the thing that creates the channel 3 signal to connect to the back of a TV) could go because modern pocket TVs use different types of signals. I removed the game switches and joystick ports and rewired them as built-in controls on the front of the unit. By the time I had finished, the 10"x5" motherboard had been reduced to just a 4"x4" square.

A big challenge was getting the Atari 2600 to output a modern composite video signal that a pocket TV could use as an input. (Composite video is the kind that's found on the yellow video cables you might use with your DVD player or VCR.) There were a few tutorials on the internet for doing this, but they didn't work quite right, so in the end I used some of the info I'd gleaned, along with a few additions of my own (like adjustable dials to tune in the correct color/levels) to get good-looking results.

Now that I'd shrunk the motherboard and got the video to work, the next step was to design a custom case. I measured all the parts (including the batteries, controller buttons, and the Casio 2.5" pocket TV I used for a display) and then modeled them on Adobe Illustrator. This allowed me to move everything around and change the layout until A) things fit properly, and B) the unit looked cool!

Once the case was designed, I cut it using a CNC (computer numerically controlled) machine. Using a variety of drill bits, the machine automatically carved the case out of solid pieces of acrylic (basically, inch-thick plexiglass), based on the computer drawings I had done. I painted the case and stuffed it with the Atari guts, the game controls (directional pad and trigger), and the pocket TV. Then I screwed the case parts together. I designed the graphics to describe controls and decorate the unit, and thermally printed them on the package.

Finally, I applied thin, adhesive-backed woodgrain to add that 1970s-era touch!

Since building my original portable Atari 2600 videogame system, I have also built portable versions of the NES, SNES, Sega Genesis, and both PlayStation 1 and 2 using these same techniques.

At the end of 1999, I wandered into a used game store and noticed they had quite a selection of Atari 2600 games. I asked the clerk if people still bought that old stuff. He informed me that yes, indeed, it was still quite popular.

Upon learning that I wasn't the last Atari 2600 fan on the planet, I though it'd be cool if I built a project to honor the old system. After some internet research, I learned that the guts of the 2600 were quite simple. I decided to make a portable version.

The first step was to cut off any unneeded portions of the motherboard. I followed the circuit board traces to determine what could and could not be removed.

Do you have your own Homebrew story to share? Send it to us at *homebrew@makezine.com*.